Country
Quilts
in a Day

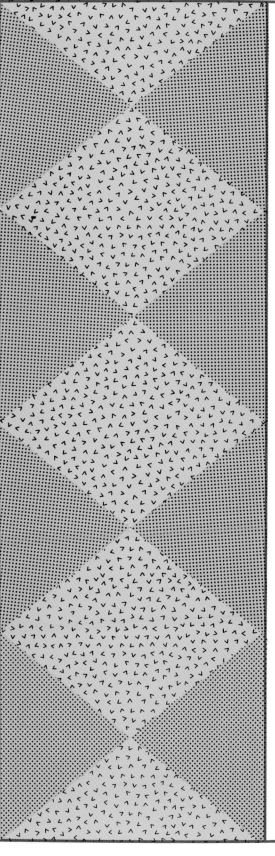

Country Quilts in a Day

Using Strip Quilting & Other Speed Techniques

Fran Roen

 Sterling Publishing Co., Inc.   New York

Edited by Claire Wilson

Library of Congress Cataloging-in-Publication Data

Roen, Fran.
    Country quilts in a day : using strip quilting and other speed
techniques / by Fran Roen.
        p.   cm.
    Includes index.
    ISBN 0-8069-8289-6. — ISBN 0-8069-8288-8 (pbk.)
    1. Machine quilting—Patterns.   2. Patchwork—Patterns.
I. Title.
TT835.R625   1991
746.9′7—dc20   91-2937
                                                    CIP

10   9   8   7   6   5   4   3   2   1

© 1991 by Fran Roen
Published by Sterling Publishing Company, Inc.
387 Park Avenue South, New York, N.Y. 10016
Distributed in Canada by Sterling Publishing
℅ Canadian Manda Group, P.O. Box 920, Station U
Toronto, Ontario, Canada M8Z 5P9
Distributed in Great Britain and Europe by Cassell PLC
Villiers House, 41/47 Strand, London WC2N 5JE, England
Distributed in Australia by Capricorn Ltd.
P.O. Box 665, Lane Cove, NSW 2066
Manufactured in the United States of America
All rights reserved

Sterling ISBN 0-8069-8289-6 Trade
                8288-8 Paper

DEDICATION

I would like to thank my best friend Jah, my wonderful husband Ron, and my beautiful children for their help and love.

Metric Equivalents

INCHES TO MILLIMETRES AND CENTIMETRES

MM—millimetres   CM—centimetres

Inches	MM	CM	Inches	CM	Inches	CM
⅛	3	0.3	9	22.9	30	76.2
¼	6	0.6	10	25.4	31	78.7
⅜	10	1.0	11	27.9	32	81.3
½	13	1.3	12	30.5	33	83.8
⅝	16	1.6	13	33.0	34	86.4
¾	19	1.9	14	35.6	35	88.9
⅞	22	2.2	15	38.1	36	91.4
1	25	2.5	16	40.6	37	94.0
1¼	32	3.2	17	43.2	38	96.5
1½	38	3.8	18	45.7	39	99.1
1¾	44	4.4	19	48.3	40	101.6
2	51	5.1	20	50.8	41	104.1
2½	64	6.4	21	53.3	42	106.7
2	76	7.6	22	55.9	43	109.2
3½	89	8.9	23	58.4	44	111.8
4	102	10.2	24	61.0	45	114.3
4½	114	11.4	25	63.5	46	116.8
5	127	12.7	26	66.0	47	119.4
6	152	15.2	27	68.6	48	121.9
7	178	17.8	28	71.1	49	124.5
8	203	20.3	29	73.7	50	127.0

CONTENTS

Introduction

I've taught and enjoyed quilting for a number of years, but have always been a bit frustrated by the amount of time that it took to complete each project. That's why I became really excited when I learned about strip quilting. With this method, you can make in a few days a beautiful quilt that looks as though you spent weeks, or even months, on it. The more I learned about strip quilting, the more excited I became, because its innovative sewing and cutting techniques were simple enough for a beginner, yet precise enough for the most seasoned of quilters. Furthermore, as a mother of eight, I greatly appreciate the speed of strip quilting as well as its simplicity, which allows me to teach my younger children the art of quilting.

The thing that makes strip quilting so fast and simple is the sewing machine. Many purists consider this technique too non-traditional, but it actually has a long and well-established history. For example, the Smithsonian Institution in Washington, D.C., has in its collections a beautiful crib quilt that was made with a sewing machine in 1879 by a Mr. Stewart Granger of Worcester, MA. A *Scientific American* article dated March 18, 1892 displays an advertisement for a sewing machine attachment made specifically for quilting. Such items provide machine quilting with a history that is more than one hundred years old—surely enough time to make it a tradition.

Quilting has always been passed on from generation to generation. As a result, it is a tradition to which new ideas and techniques are always being added. So if you should discover a shortcut or innovation during the course of your quilting, pass it on to others so that the craft can be further developed. Always be proud of your work and sign and date all the quilts that you make. You and those you give them to will enjoy them for years to come.

MATERIALS

Included in this section are suggestions for the basic necessities of quilting. If you are a first-time quilter, I would suggest using the types of materials that I discuss below. When you have become acquainted with quilting materials and their uses, you may certainly choose to try new ideas of your own.

Fabric

You can use almost any type of fabric for quilting, as long as all of your choices are of the same weight and have the same fibre content. I prefer to use cotton for the top pieces and unbleached muslin for the backing. However, if you decide to use a bedsheet for your backing, choose one that is a size larger than your quilt and remove all of its hems.

All fabric should be prewashed. The best way that I have found to do this is to fill my sink with the hottest water that I can put my hands in and then to fully immerse my lightest fabric. If the color bleeds, I let the fabric soak for a while and then wring it out, refill the sink, and start over again. If the fabric bleeds a second time, then I turn to my washing machine, fill it to the lowest level with cold water, and add a mixture of $1\frac{1}{4}$ cups of white vinegar and $\frac{1}{2}$ cup of salt (this mixture will set colors nine out of ten times). I allow the fabric to soak for at least four hours, but overnight is better when possible. If the fabric still bleeds after this process, then label your finished quilt "dry-clean only."

COLOR

There are no rules for choosing fabric color. Simply find one that you like and build your quilt around it. It might help if you try to pick a color that complements the room in which the quilt will be kept or that fits the personality of the person to whom you will give the quilt. If you are at a total loss, you can always visit your local art store and pick up a color wheel, which will show you the colors that go together best.

AMOUNT

All quilt patterns in this book are made with 45-inch-wide fabric. Yardage amounts will be given with each pattern. To determine the right size for a bed quilt, measure the bed for which it is intended when it is completely made up. Decide beforehand how far down you want the quilt to hang and whether you want it to go under or over the pillows.

If the pattern needs enlarging, increase the size of the borders or add an additional border. If the quilt will be too large, reduce the size or number of borders.

Batting

Cotton batting is traditional and very nice to work with, but it is often not readily available. Polyester batting is much more common and is easier to care for as well. If you are going to tie your quilt together, then use bonded polyester batting because it will hold its shape better in the washing machine. If you plan to hand- or machine-quilt your pieces together, then regular unbonded batting will be fine. Your quilting stitches will hold the batting in place.

Thread

Cotton thread is best, but it is often hard to come by. Cotton-covered polyester thread is much more readily available and works equally as well. Whatever you choose, remember that you want your quilt to last, so always select the best-quality thread that you can afford.

Needles

If you plan to quilt by hand, then I suggest using a #7 or #8 needle. If you are going to quilt on a sewing machine, then use a #14 or #16 machine needle. Also, if you plan to tie your quilt instead of sewing a quilting pattern, use a large-eye needle and good-quality yarn or embroidery floss.

Sewing Machine

Any well-running sewing machine will do. If you also have a surger, I would suggest using it, but you can get along just fine without one. Always make sure that your machine is well-oiled, the thread tension is on the correct setting, and everything is running smoothly. Nothing seems to stop a project as fast as a poorly running machine. Unfortunately, most of those stopped projects never seem to get finished.

Rotary Cutter

After the sewing machine, this tool is one of the most important aids to speedy quilting. Rotary cutters are generally sold in two sizes—small and large. I recommend the smaller size because I find that it is easier to handle and requires less pressure when cutting. Remember when using this tool always to place a mat or cutting board underneath your fabric before cutting. Otherwise, your work surface will become badly scored and your blade will dull quickly.

Scissors

It's always a good idea to keep a pair of sharp scissors next to your machine. That way, you can cut off small threads right away instead of having to go back and do it later.

Pins

Extra-long quilting pins are the most practical type to use for these projects. You will also want to have a number of large safety pins on hand if you are going to machine quilt. It will take approximately 20 to 24 dozen pins to put together a king-size quilt.

Ruler

Most of the patterns in this book require 2½ inch strips, so I went to my local hardware store and had them cut me a piece of Plexiglas that measures 2½ inches × 27 inches (I made sure that it measured 2½ inches across down its full length before I left the store). The best thing to use for quilting is an acrylic ruler, but these can be expensive. Plexiglas is a very affordable alternative—my piece cost less than two dollars.

Marking Pen

For some of the patterns, you will have to draw a grid on the back of your fabric. I use a washable pen or pencil, either of which can be purchased in stores that sell sewing supplies. You can even use a fine-line ballpoint pen because the lines will disappear if you cut exactly along them.

Iron

I strongly suggest keeping your iron on hand and ready when you are sewing your quilt pieces together. It is much easier to connect subsequent pieces when the seams on the first ones are pressed down.

Seam Ripper

We are all imperfect and this tool allows us to get rid of our mistakes quickly and cleanly. Mine is always nearby.

SPEED TECHNIQUES

Your first speed technique will be to cut all of your quilt pieces with the rotary cutter. Indeed, this tool will reduce your cutting time by at least seventy-five percent. It seems that I always have at least one student in my classes who is not willing to try this tool. That student will go home and cut out her fabric the traditional way—with scissors—over the course of about four or five hours. The rest of the students will use the rotary cutter and get their work done in an hour or less.

Using the Rotary Cutter: Lay your cutting mat or board down on your work surface. Then lay down your first piece of fabric so that the grain is vertical to you. (All strips are cut with the grain.) Now lay down the rest of your fabrics, one on top of the other and with all the grains aligned. It is best not to try to cut through more than six pieces of fabric at a time, and remember that the more fabric you cut, the greater the pressure that you must apply to the rotary cutter. If you are right-handed, you should start cutting your strips on the left side of the fabric and work toward the right. If you are left-handed, do the opposite.

Before you cut your first strip, trim all of the edges of your fabric pile so that the edges line up. Then, using your ruler, measure in 2½ inches from the edge, press down firmly on your ruler, and run your rotary cutter along the edge of the ruler. If you don't cut through all of the layers on the first pass, go back and finish with your scissors. As you become more experienced, you will learn to apply the right amount of pressure and avoid this problem.

When you have finished cutting your strips, it will be time to use the next speed technique—strip sewing. To do this, choose a pair of strips in complementary colors, then place strips of one color face down on top of the face-up strips of the other color. Repeat this with as many sets of colors as you have, according to the directions in each pattern. Sew your first pair of strips together but do not cut them loose from the sewing machine. Simply butt in the next set of strips (Illus. 2) and continue with the rest of the pairs until they are all sewn together. This will save you a great deal of time.

Several quilt patterns call for a large number of half-square triangles—that is, triangles that form a square when two are joined along their longest side. There is a speed technique that will allow you to quickly sew many sets of these triangles. It is done by reversing the usual practice—you sew the triangles together to form squares first and then cut them out.

To start, make a grid on the back of your darkest fabric. If your finished square is supposed to measure four inches, then your grid should consist of five-inch squares in order to leave a seam allowance. After you have drawn this grid, draw a diagonal line through each of the squares (Illus. 2).

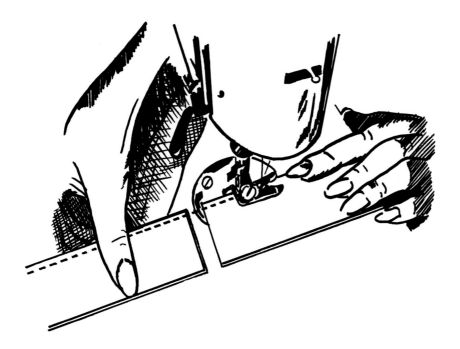

Illus. 1. Strip sewing.

Next, lay your fabric facedown on a piece of fabric of a complementary light color. Now you are ready to sew your triangles. Line your fabric up on your sewing machine so that the needle is one quarter inch from the first diagonal line and sew the length of the line, but make sure that you pick up the needle each time you come to the point of another triangle. Do not sew through it. When you have finished the first line, turn your fabric 180 degrees and sew along the other side of the first diagonal line, making sure to leave a one-quarter-inch seam allowance. When

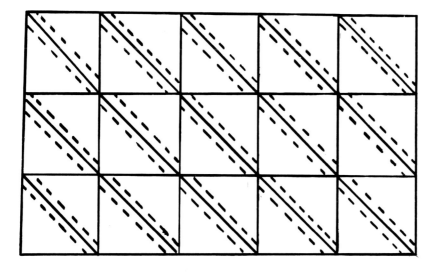

Illus. 2. Speedy triangle sewing.

15

you have sewn along both sides of all the diagonal lines, then cut along the outlines of the squares and along the diagonal lines. Your triangles are now ready to be pieced together for your quilt.

MACHINE TYING

This is the fastest method of joining your quilt pieces together. To begin, mark your quilt at each tie-point. These should occur every four to six inches if you are using polyester batting, but you should tie every two to three inches if you use cotton batting. Always work on a flat surface and always begin marking your tie-points at the middle of your quilt.

Next, pin all three layers of your quilt before you begin sewing. It may be helpful to tape your backing to the floor while pinning in order to keep it from shifting. Always start your pinning from the middle and work out towards the edges. Make sure that you pin around the tie-points and not on top of them.

When you have finished pinning, roll the sides of your quilt in towards the middle. This will make it easier for you to maneuver the quilt on your sewing machine. In order to machine-tie your quilt, you should lower your feed-dogs, use your regular presser foot and tension, and set your machine for its widest zigzag stitch. Start sewing at the center of your quilt and work out towards the edges. Pull both ends of a piece of yarn through the first tie point and make a knot or bow. Then lower the presser foot and zigzag over the center of the tie—this is called bar-tacking. Move to your next tie point and make another yarn knot or bow and another bar-tack. When you are finished, clip the loose threads and remove all of the pins.

DIAGONAL QUILTING BY MACHINE

The first step is to mark the quilting pattern on your work. If it is a small piece, such as a wall hanging or a place mat, then mark lines every two inches. For larger projects, such as bed coverings, mark the lines every five or six inches.

Start your marking on the bias of the fabric. To find this, place your quilt on a flat surface so that the grain is vertical to you. Next, fold the righthand corner over toward the left until the grain on the folded piece is perpendicular to the grain on the fabric underneath (Illus. 3). Press lightly along the fold to create a guideline. Then open the fold, take a ruler, and mark

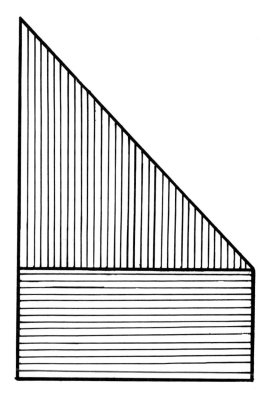

Illus. 3. Finding the bias.

each line with erasable pen or pencil at the appropriate distance. When you have marked the entire quilt, turn it over and mark the other side in the same way. You should end up with a diamond pattern on both sides. Finally, pin all three layers of fabric together, making sure that they are secure.

Start sewing at the upper-lefthand corner and move towards the lower-righthand corner. This is a spiralling technique, so start with most of your quilt to the left of the machine. When you have finished your first line, leave the needle in the fabric, raise the presser foot, and turn your quilt 90 degrees. Move your quilt over so that the needle rests on the second line, lower the presser foot, and sew the length of the line. Repeat this until you have finished the entire top side of your quilt. Then flip it over and sew the back side in the same manner. When you are

17

done with the back, turn the quilt over again and sew the lines that run perpendicular to the ones that you sewed before. Repeat on the back until the entire quilt is done (see Illus. 4).

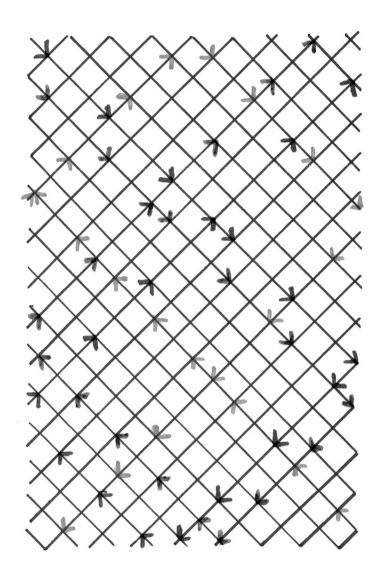

Illus. 4. Diagonal quilting by machine.

BACKING YOUR QUILT

I have three favorite ways of backing my quilts. One is to lay the backing down wrong side up, lay the batting on top of it, and the quilt on top of that. Then I trim the batting to fit the quilt and the backing to two inches larger around than the quilt.

I then fold the back over the batting and tuck it under the quilt and then pin and sew the front and back together.

Another backing method I like that is very fast and easy is the pillow case method. To begin, lay your batting down on the floor, then your backing face-up, and your quilt face-down on top of the backing. Pin and sew the edges of all three layers, with your machine set for ten to twelve stitches per inch. Sew all the way around except for a three-foot opening on one side. Cut your quilt free from the machine and trim the batting close to the stitching. Roll the corners and sides tightly towards the opening and pull the whole quilt through the hole. Flatten your quilt and slip stitch the opening.

Finally, there is bias binding. For this method, use fabric that blends well with the quilt top because it will serve as a binding. The size of the quilt will determine the width of the binding. For a small crib quilt, you will use a small, narrow binding. For a large quilt, you'll need a wider binding. Sew the binding first to the top of the quilt and then fold it over to the back. Tuck the raw edge underneath and slip stitch.

HELPFUL HINTS

- For a beautifully finished quilt, take time to cut, sew, and press your pieces accurately.
- When quilting, always use a quarter-inch seam allowance.
- Always set your machine for 10 to 12 stitches per inch.
- When pressing seams, press them towards the darkest fabric to avoid a shadow behind light colors.
- When joining two pieces that already have seams, sew in opposite directions to avoid bulk.
- Always prewash your fabrics.

Now comes the hard part—choosing a pattern.

1
Irish Chain

The basic pattern for Irish Chain will give you a plain but attractive quilt. However, by changing the placement of the plain and nine-block squares, you can create interesting and varied designs.

YARDAGE

2¾ yards of medium shade, medium-size floral print fabric
5½ yards of light shade, small-size floral print fabric.

CUTTING

Please read "Speed Techniques" and "Rotary Cutter" in the front of this book before you start.

Medium shade	cut fifteen strips at 3½ × 45 inches
	cut eight strips at 5 × 45 inches
Light shade	cut twelve strips at 3½ × 45 inches
	cut eight strips at 4 × 45 inches
	cut thirty-one squares at 10½ × 10½ inches

SEWING INSTRUCTIONS

Lay a 3½-inch medium strip faceup on your machine, lay a 3½-inch light shade on top of it, and sew the two together. Then sew a second 3½-inch medium strip to the other side as in Illus. 1–1. Sew five more of these sets.

Then sew 3 sets of 3½-inch strips in a light-medium-light combination, as indicated in Illus. 1–2. Press the seams on all of the sets.

Measure down 3½ inches on one of the sets and cut. Repeat this step with the rest of that strip and with all the others. Sew the sections together to form a nine-block square (see Illus. 1–3). Sew 32 of these blocks.

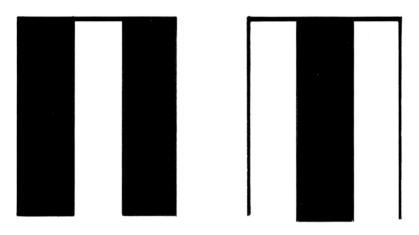

Illus. 1–1 and 1–2. Strip patterns.

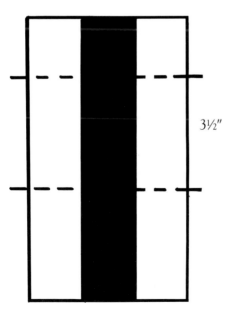

3½"

Illus. 1–3. Cutting to make the blocks.

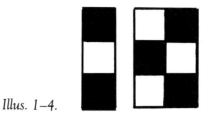

Illus. 1–4.

Arrange the nine-block squares and the plain squares according to Illus. 1–4 so that there are seven blocks across and nine blocks down.

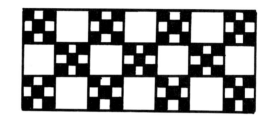

Illus. 1–5.

Sew the short ends of pairs of your 4×45-inch strips together to form 90-inch strips. Do the same with the 5×45-inch strips. Apply the 4-inch strips to the top and bottom and then to the sides of your quilt. Repeat with the 5-inch strips.

2
Rainbow

You'll need fabric in nine colors for Rainbow. Like Trip Around the World (p. 67), this pattern looks complex but requires very little actual work.

YARDAGE

Light color A	¾ yard
Light color B	¾ yard
Medium light color A	¾ yard
Medium light color B	¾ yard
Medium color A	¾ yard
Medium color B	¾ yard
Medium dark color A	¾ yard
Medium dark color B	¾ yard
Dark color	¾ yard
First border	¾ yard
Second border	1 yard
Third border	1½ yards

CUTTING

Please read "Speed Techniques" and "Rotary Cutter" in the front of this book before you start.

All colors	cut four strips at 4×45 inches
First border	cut eight strips at 3×45 inches
Second border	cut eight strips at 4×45 inches
Third border	cut eight strips at 5×45 inches

No Tupperware parties for our foremothers. Instead, they enjoyed day-long quilting parties. During winter days, when little outdoor work could be done, groups of women would congregate at a neighbor's home, set up a quilting frame, and work and talk until dusk, as their children played around them.

The women usually stuffed their quilts with bits of old blankets or coats, but if they ran out, they used straw, hay, or corn husks. They had to use whatever was handy.

26

SEWING INSTRUCTIONS

Sew four sets of strips arranged in the following order:

Medium dark color A
Medium color A
Medium light color A
Light color A
Light color B
Medium light color B
Medium color B
Medium dark color B
Dark color

You may reverse the order of matching color types if you want—for example, switch the order of the two medium light colors. Press your sets so that the seams are toward the darkest color. Place the sheets on a flat surface with the medium dark end strip on top and mark vertical cutting lines every 4 inches across the set of strips. Cut the sets to form strips of different colored

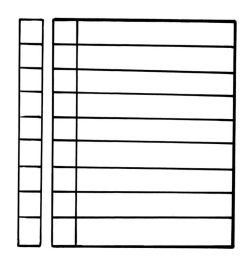

Illus. 2–1.

squares (Illus. 2–1). You will need to make four sheets of squares to form your quilt top—two of eight strips, which we will call Sheet 1 and Sheet 3, and two of nine strips, which we will call Sheet 2 and Sheet 4. You will have leftovers from making your sheets that you should save for the border.

To start, lay down Sheet 1 so that the colored strips align. You will be sewing each strip back to one that it was cut apart from but first you have to rearrange the colors. First, cut the top square from the second strip and sew it to the bottom of that strip. Continue this process by cutting off the required number of squares from each strip and sewing them back onto the bottoms of those strips, as shown in Illus. 2–2. Repeat this process for Sheet 3. Next, follow the diagram in Illus. 2–3 to sew Sheet 2 and Sheet 4 in the proper order.

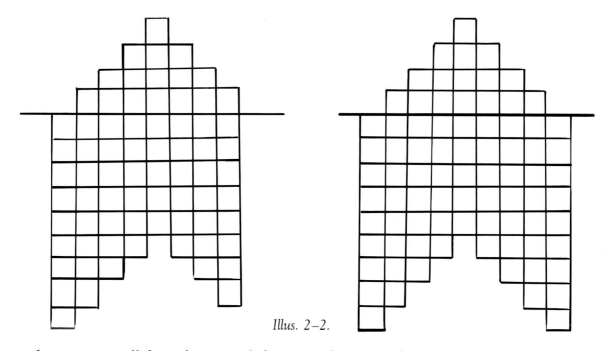

Illus. 2–2.

Press the seams in all four sheets and then sew them together according to the diagram in Illus. 2–4. Then press again and add the first, second, and third borders. Finish the quilt by whatever method you prefer.

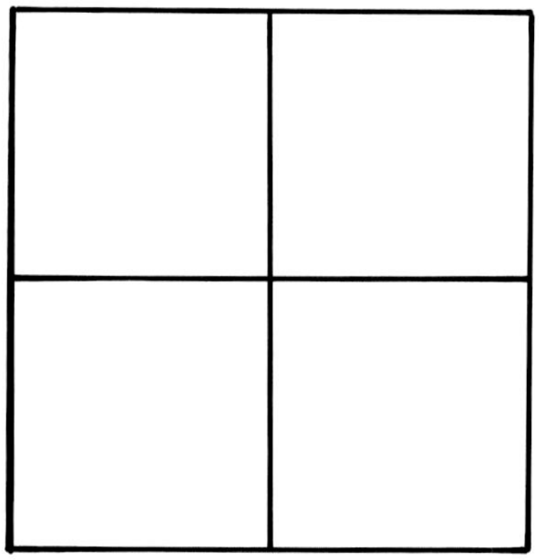

Illus. 2–3.

29

30

3
Log Cabin

The colors that quilters choose when making this pattern are sometimes used to symbolize certain feelings or beliefs. For example, when the "log cabin" blocks have red centers, they honor the warmth and love of family togetherness, and when they have yellow centers, they indicate hospitality and welcome to strangers. According to tradition, each block should have a dark side to represent the sadder times of life and a light side to stand for the happier times.

YARDAGE

Center squares	¼ yard
Light color A	½ yard plus ¾ yard for border
Light color B	⅔ yard
Light color C	1 yard plus 1 yard for border
Dark color A	⅝ yard
Dark color B	1 yard plus 1½ yards for border
Dark color C	1½ yards
Backing	5½ yards
First border	¾ yard
Second border	1 yard
Third border	1½ yards

CUTTING

Please read "Speed Techniques" and "Rotary Cutter" in the front of this book.

Center square	cut two strips at 2×45 inches
Light color A	cut four strips at 2×45 inches
Light color B	cut eight strips at 2×45 inches
Light color C	cut twelve strips at 2×45 inches
Dark color A	cut six strips at 2×45 inches
Dark color B	cut nine strips at 2×45 inches
Dark color C	cut fourteen strips at 2×45 inches
First border	cut eight strips at 3×45 inches
Second border	cut eight strips at $4^{1/2} \times 45$ inches
Third border	cut ten strips at 6×45 inches

SEWING INSTRUCTIONS

For this project, every color except that for the center square will be used twice. First, cut your center strip into 2-inch squares (Illus. 3–1). When finished, you should have a total of twenty-four 2×2-inch squares. Next, lay a strip of light color A faceup onto your sewing machine and begin sewing the 2-inch squares onto it; remember to place them face down onto the strip. Continue sewing until you have attached all of your squares. Cut apart your blocks (Illus. 3–2).

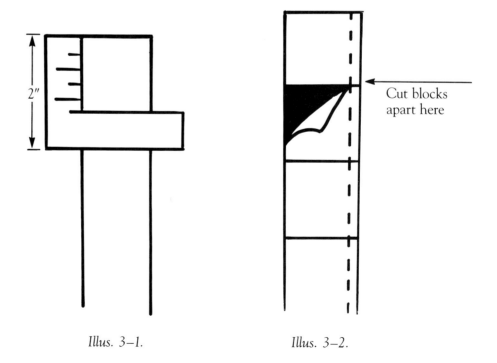

Illus. 3–1.   Illus. 3–2.

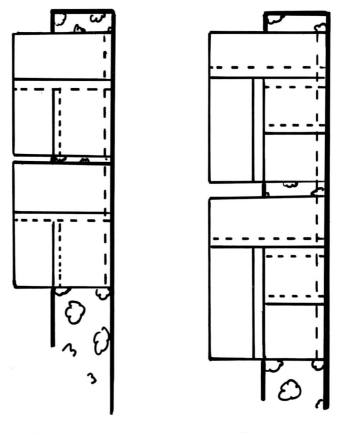

Illus. 3–3.   Illus. 3–4.

Take another strip of light color A and lay it faceup on your machine. Then take one of your blocks and lay it facedown and lengthwise on the strip, making sure that the light strip added in the last step is on the top. Sew along the 4-inch length of the block. Butt in the next block and sew in the same manner. Do the same with the rest of your blocks, adding strips as necessary.

Lay a strip of dark color A faceup on your machine and lay a block facedown on top of it. Again, make sure that the last strip of light color A is at the top of the block (Illus. 3–3). Follow the same sewing steps until you have completed all the blocks. Then do the same with a second strip of dark color A.

Attach the rest of your strips (remember to use each color twice) in the following order: light color B (2×), dark color B (2×), light color C (2×), dark color C (2×). When all of your strips have been added to the blocks, sew them together in the pattern shown in the drawing on page 33.

Finally, you must add the borders. First sew together pairs of the border strips at their short ends. Then add the first border to the sides of your quilt and then to the top and bottom. Do the same with the second and third borders. Finish the quilt using whichever method you prefer.

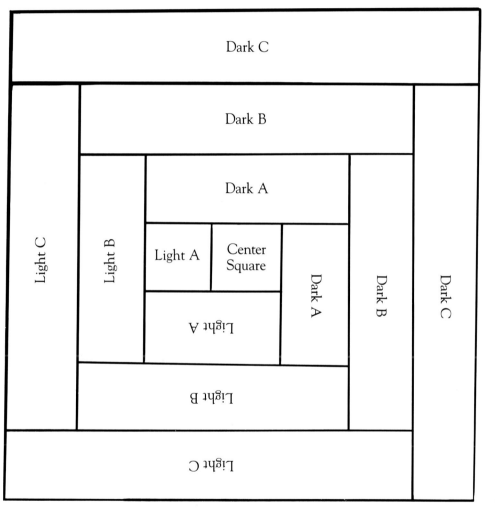

Illus. 3–5.

4
Star Burst

You will need fabric in five colors for this project—four for the star burst and one for the background. You should also keep in mind that, if you want your quilt to be larger than 66×66 inches, you will have to add borders. For these, you should choose colors that complement your quilt. The lettered colors below indicate yardage for each color from light to dark, with A being the lightest.

YARDAGE

Color A	¾ yard
Color B	1½ yards
Color C	1⅞ yards (center and points of your star)
Color D	1½ yards
Background color	2¾ yards
Backing (no borders)	6 yards

Borders for 90 × 90 inch quilt:

First border	¾ yard
Second border	1 yard
Third border	1½ yards

Borders for 96 × 96 inch quilt:

First border	1 yard
Second border	1¼ yards
Third border	2 yards

CUTTING

Please read "Speed Techniques" and "Rotary Cutter" in the front of this book before you start.

Color A	cut eight strips at $2\frac{1}{2} \times 45$ inches
Color B	cut sixteen strips at $2\frac{1}{2} \times 45$ inches
Color C	cut twenty-four strips at $2\frac{1}{2} \times 45$ inches
Color D	cut sixteen strips at $2\frac{1}{2} \times 45$ inches
Background color	cut twenty $11\frac{1}{2}$-inch squares
	cut four 12-inch squares and cut them in half diagonally

90×90-inch quilt:

First border	cut eight 3×45-inch strips
Second border	cut eight 4×45-inch strips
Third border	cut eight 5×45-inch strips

96×96-inch quilt:

First border	cut eight 4×45-inch strips
Second border	cut eight 5×45-inch strips
Third border	cut nine 6×45-inch strips

SEWING INSTRUCTIONS

Before sewing your strips, please read "Speed Techniques" in the front of this book. Then refer to Illus. 4–1 and Illus. 4–2 to determine the placement of your strips. The illustrations show the amount of space that you should leave from the end of each preceding strip when you add another. Sew them one at a time into sets of four until you have eight sets of each group. Remember to carefully press all of the seams toward the darkest color.

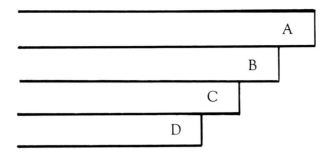

Illus. 4–1.

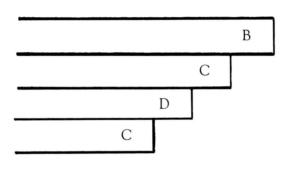

Illus. 4–2.

Next, cut new strips from the sets that you have just sewn. First mark the sets of strips with diagonal lines, as shown in Illus. 4–3. The strips should each measure 2½ inches wide and you should be able to get about 16 strips from each fabric block. If you can't, don't worry! This is a generous pattern and you should have leftovers.

Your next step will be to join the newly created strips together in sets of four to form diamonds. These will be the points of your star burst. Sew thirty-two individual diamonds in the combination indicated in Illus. 4–4. Then join four of the diamonds together along their sides, making sure that the colors on each match up as in the photograph and drawing. Join a second set of four diamonds together and join these to the first set. This will form the center star in your quilt. Then sew eight of your squares to the upper sides of your diamonds.

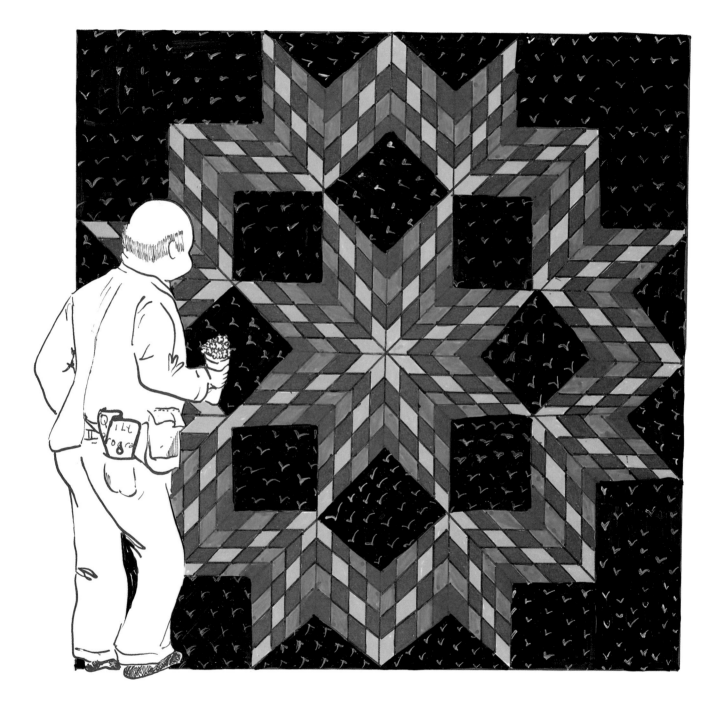

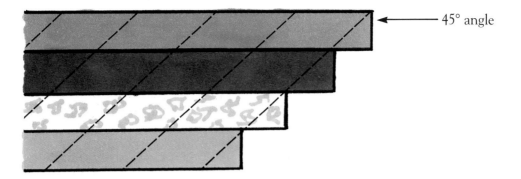

45° angle

Illus. 4–3.

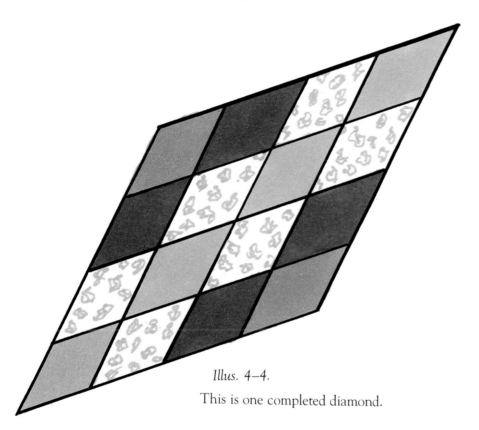

Illus. 4–4.

This is one completed diamond.

Next, sew three diamonds together to form a burst—you should make eight of these. Attach these bursts to the free sides of the squares that you added in the last step.

Now you can sew your background-color triangles to the sides, top, and bottom of your diamonds, as shown in the illustration and photograph. Then attach your remaining squares to form the corners of your quilt.

Finish your quilt using whichever method you prefer.

STAR BURST WORKSHEET

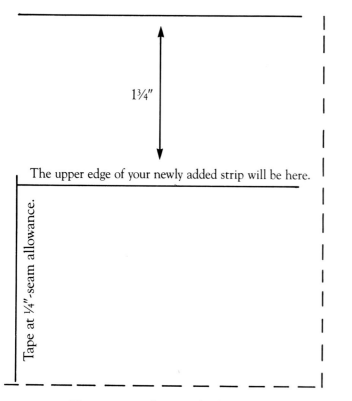

1¾″

The upper edge of your newly added strip will be here.

Tape at ¼″-seam allowance.

Photocopy and cut on broken line.

A

B

C

D

Pin a small swatch of fabric next to its letter.

45-degree angle guide.

5
Shadow Box

This pattern is most often used by and usually associated with Amish quilters. You will need four light-colored fabrics and one dark fabric for this project, as indicated in the photograph and drawing.

YARDAGE

Light colors A–D	1 yard
Dark color	2½ yards
Backing	6½ yards

CUTTING

Please read "Speed Techniques" and "Rotary Cutter" in the front of this book before you start.

Light colors A–D	cut ten strips at 2½ × 45 inches
Dark color	cut twenty squares at 12 × 12 inches, then cut in half to get forty half-square triangles

SEWING INSTRUCTIONS

Sew your light strips together in combinations of four so that they are arranged from lightest to darkest (Illus. 5–1). When done, you will have ten blocks of strips.

MORE QUILTS

Next, press the seams toward the darkest color. Then lay the fabric combinations faceup and mark triangles on them, as indicated in Illus. 5–2.

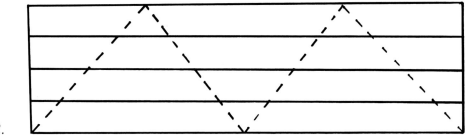

Illus. 5–2.

When you have cut all the triangles, sew together a striped and a solid triangle along the longest sides. Complete the rest of your blocks in this way and then arrange and sew them in whatever pattern you like (see Illus. 5–4 for an example).

Illus. 5–3.

Illus. 5–4.

48

6
Reversible Window

This is a reversible quilt, so you will need to buy the same amounts of fabric for both sides. However, you should buy them in different colors to create a different quilt for each side. Although either side can be the front of this quilt, I will label one side as "Front" and the other as "Back" so as to avoid confusion in the instructions.

When making this pattern, I always load three bobbins with thread. When the third bobbin is empty, I clean and oil my machine, making sure to remove the batting lint from the feed-dog and bobbin areas. This only takes a few minutes and can save your machine. You can use up a great deal of your leftover batting in this project; just make sure that it is all the same weight.

YARDAGE

Light color	1 yard each for Front and Back
Medium light color	1 yard each for Front and Back
Medium color	1¾ yards each for Front and Back
Dark color	2½ yards each for Front and Back
First border	¾ yard each for Front and Back
Second border	1 yard each for Front and Back
Third border	1½ yards each for Front and Back
Batting	81 × 96 inches of batting (or equivalent of leftover batting)

CUTTING

(Follow cutting instructions two times—once for each side of the quilt.)

Light color	cut two strips at 3×45 inches
Medium light color	cut ten strips at 2½×45 inches
Medium color	cut seventeen strips at 2½×45 inches
Dark color	cut twenty-six strips at 2½×45 inches
First border	cut eight strips at 3×45 inches
Second border	cut eight strips at 4×45 inches
Third border	cut eight strips at 5×45 inches
Batting	cut ten strips at 3×45 inches
	cut one hundred and six strips at 2½×45 inches
	cut eight strips at 4×45 inches
	cut eight strips at 5×45 inches

SEWING INSTRUCTIONS

Place a 3-inch strip of batting on the machine. Then take a 3-inch strip of Front light fabric and place it faceup on top of the batting. Next, place a 3-inch strip of Back light fabric facedown on the top of the Front fabric (Illus 6–1). Sew down the length of the strips. When it is finished, cut the piece free from the machine and fold the Back strip over the batting. Then sew the Front and Back fabrics together (Illus. 6–2). Do the same with the rest of the two sets of 3-inch light strips. When finished, measure 3 inches down your first sewn strip and cut. Repeat this process until you have twenty 3-inch squares.

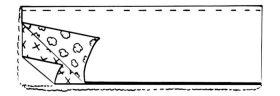

Illus. 6–1.

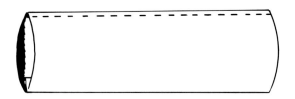

Illus. 6–2.

In every town, there was one person who stood out as the "master" quilter. Such a person often had her, and sometimes his, own collection of patterns. As the master quilter neared the end of her life, she would put together a quilt that contained sample blocks of all of her favorite patterns, so that they might be passed on. This is the origin of the Sampler quilt.

When sewing the rest of the quilt, remember to always have the same color on top. This will help you to avoid quite a few mistakes. I know it has kept me from having to rip out seams many times.

Next, lay a 2½-inch batting strip on your machine. Then place a 2½-inch strip of medium light Front fabric faceup on top of the batting and a block from the last step on top of the medium light fabric so that both pieces of Front fabric face each other. Last lay a 2½-inch medium light Back strip facedown on top of the block.

You are now about to sew a "Dagwood" sandwich, so to speak, consisting of: batting—Front strip—3×3 block—Back strip (Illus. 6–3). Sew through everything until you are at the end of the block. Then pick up your Back strip and butt in another block underneath it, making sure that everything stays lined up. Sew to the end of the second block and then butt in the next one, repeating the process until all twenty of your blocks are finished.

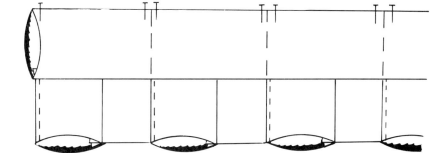

Illus. 6–3.

Next, take your strips with the finished blocks and, before you cut them apart, fold over the Back fabric and sew it to the Front fabric, encasing the batting. You will not repeat this step with the rest of the instructions. Instead, you'll use pins to anchor your seams. When all the strips are sewn, you can cut apart your blocks.

Next, make another sandwich with 2½-inch batting strip, 2½-inch medium light Front strip, a block with the previously added strip at the top, and a 2½-inch, medium light Back strip. Make sure that the two Front strips line up and that the Back strip is facedown. Sew through everything and butt in new blocks and add new strips as necessary.

When you have finished sewing, lay your sewn strips on your cutting board with the Front fabric on the bottom. Fold the

Back fabric over the batting and pin the edge to the Front fabric edge. Then cut apart the blocks.

Continue to add your medium light colors in this manner until your center square is completely surrounded. Then add your medium and then your dark Front and Back colors in the same manner. When you are finished, your square should look like that pictured in Illus. 6–4.

To connect your blocks, push a dark Front strip and batting toward the body of block. Then do the same with a second block, and lay it on top of the first so that the Front and Back fabrics have their right sides facing. Then sew the two blocks together (Illus. 6–5). Do the same with the rest of the blocks, both Front and Back, making five sets of four blocks. Then sew your rows of four together to make five rows.

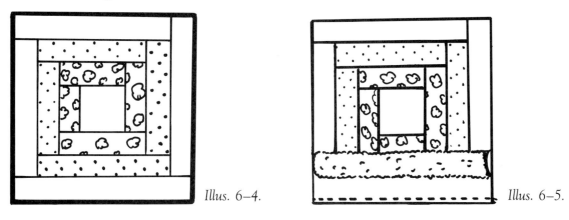

Illus. 6–4.   Illus. 6–5.

Now you can add your borders. Take two 3 × 45-inch, first border strips and sew two of their short ends together. Do the same with the rest of the strips. Then sew your 3 × 45-inch batting strips together in the same manner. Lay your batting on the machine and lay a Front first border strip faceup on top of it. Next, place a row of your blocks on top with the Front fabric facedown on top of the Front border strip. Last, place the Back first border strip facedown on the rest. Sew the length of your sewn blocks. Note that this quilt will be very heavy, so you should have some way to support it as you sew.

Next, fold the Back fabric over the batting, pull the Front fabric even with it, and sew the length of the first border. Repeat this process for the rest of the first border and for the second and third borders. Then your quilt is finished! This is a beautiful quilt and not really very hard. This method can also be used with the Log Cabin and Courthouse Steps patterns.

54

7
Waves

The pattern for Waves originated with New England quilters, who lived in close relation to the sea. The triangular pieces are meant to mimic the movement of the ocean.

YARDAGE

Dark color	¾ yard
Light color	1½ yards
Medium color	4 yards
Medium dark color	1½ yards
First border	¾ yard
Second border	1 yard
Third border	1½ yards

CUTTING

Please read "Speed Techniques" and "Rotary Cutter" in the front of this book before you start.

Dark color	cut twenty-four squares at 6×6 inches
Light color	cut fifteen strips at 2½×45 inches
Medium color	cut twelve strips at 2½×45 inches
	cut three strips at 4×45 inches
Medium dark color	cut fifteen strips at 2½×45 inches
First border	cut eight strips at 3×45 inches
Second border	cut eight strips at 4×45 inches
Third border	cut eight strips at 5×45 inches

SEWING INSTRUCTIONS

Sew together twelve sets of your 2½-inch strips in groups of three, going from light to dark (Illus. 7–1). Press the fabric combinations with the seams toward the darkest color. Then lay a set down faceup and horizontally and mark 2½-inch cutting lines across the length of the set (Illus. 7–2). Repeat with the rest of the set and put them aside. This group of strips will be called Group 1.

Next, sew the rest of your 2½-inch dark and light strips to either side of the 4-inch medium strips (Illus. 7–3). Press the combinations well, lay them faceup, and cut them into 2½-inch strips (Illus. 7–4). This group of strips will be called Group 2.

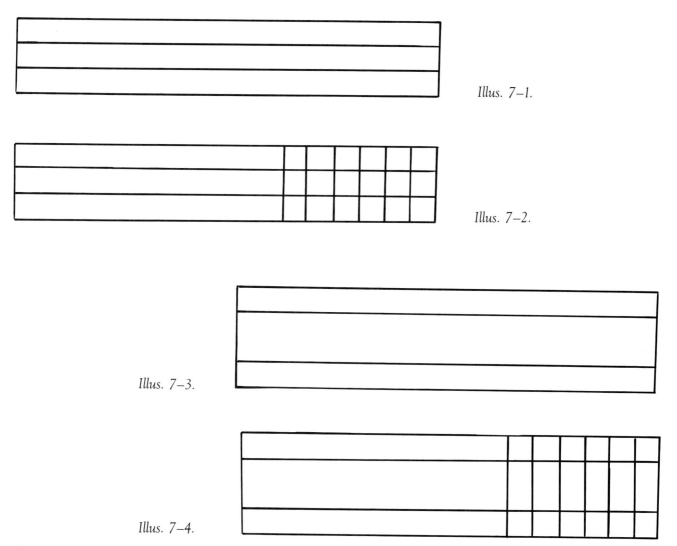

Illus. 7–1.

Illus. 7–2.

Illus. 7–3.

Illus. 7–4.

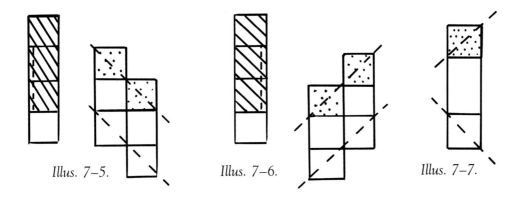

Illus. 7–5.   Illus. 7–6.   Illus. 7–7.

Divide the Group 1 sets in half. Sew one set according to the diagrams in Illus. 7–5. Sew the other set according to the diagrams in Illus. 7–6. Press the seams. Then cut the sets diagonally as indicated in Illus. 7–5 and 7–6, making sure that the same color is on top in both sets. Save the corners.

Next, you will cut the strips in Group 2. First cut the strips according to the diagram in Illus. 7–7. Save the corners. Make sure that you cut the strips so that the colors are in the same position on their tops and bottoms and in the same position as the tops and bottoms of the strips in Group 1.

Now you are ready to sew your corners together. In all, you will need forty-eight dark and forty-eight light triangles. Next, lay two triangles one on top of the other and right faces together. Arrange them according to Illus. 7–8 and make sure that the dark color is on the bottom.

You now have all the pieces to construct your blocks. First, take a 6-inch square and attach a piece from Group 1 (Illus. 7–9) with the light triangles toward the square. Make sure that you leave a ¼-inch seam allowance on the strips at either end of the square. Then do the same with another piece from Group 1, but this time sew the dark triangles next to the square (Illus. 7–10).

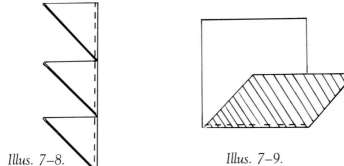

Illus. 7–8.   Illus. 7–9.

In days gone by, quilt borders were carefully plotted out so that they would be unbroken. To have a broken border was considered an omen of a troubled future, such as a marriage ended through death or disaster.

Next, sew a strip from Group 2 to the edges of the strips in Group 1 (Illus. 7–11). Press your seams toward the middle of the square.

Now repeat, adding strips from Group 1 to the remaining two sides of the square (Illus. 7–12). Remember to put light triangles opposite light triangles and dark triangles opposite dark triangles. Add corner triangles (Illus. 7–13). Repeat the whole process until you have twenty-four squares and then sew them together to form your quilt top.

Attach your first border to the sides and then to the top of your quilt and do the same with the second and third borders. Finish your quilt using whichever method you prefer.

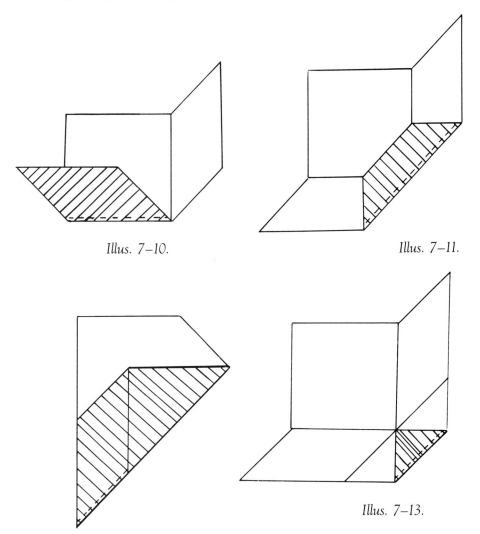

Illus. 7–10.

Illus. 7–11.

Illus. 7–12.

Illus. 7–13.

8
Double Windmill

Although Double Windmill uses only two colors, it is a very lively, interesting pattern, particularly when the fabrics have contrasting prints.

YARDAGE

Color A	2½ yards (should be dark)
Color B	2¼ yards (should be light, includes yardage for first border)
Second border	1 yard
Third border	1½ yards

CUTTING

Please read "Speed Techniques" and "Rotary Cutter" in the front of this book before you start.

Color A	cut seventeen strips at 3 × 45 inches
	cut eight strips at 4 × 45 inches
Color B	cut twelve strips at 3 × 45 inches
	cut eight strips at 4 × 45 inches (for first border)
Second border	cut eight strips at 4½ × 45 inches
Third border	cut five strips at 5 × 45 inches

During colonial times, quilts were so important that they were listed in wills and marriage inventories in great detail.

SEWING INSTRUCTIONS

Pair off a 3-inch strip of Color A and a 3-inch strip of Color B with right sides facing and sew together lengthwise along one side. Set this set aside and do the same with the rest of the 3-inch strips. You should end up with 12 sets of strips.

Lay one set of strips faceup on your cutting mat so that it is horizontal to you and Color A is on top. Then lay a second set of strips facedown on the first so that the strips of Colors A and B match up (Illus. 8–1). Measure the width of your sewn strips—it should be 5½ inches. Then measure 5½ inches along the length of the strip and cut to make a perfect square. It must be perfect for this quilt pattern to work out correctly, so if your strips are wider than 5½ inches, then cut the square to match the width. You should get about six or seven squares per set.

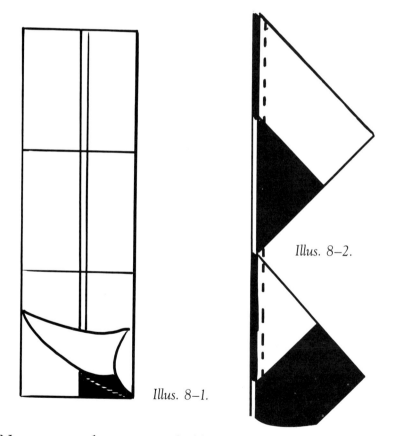

Illus. 8–2.

Illus. 8–1.

Next, cut each square in half on its diagonal and sew the cut triangles together so that opposites face one another (Illus. 8–2). Because you will be sewing along the bias, be careful not to stretch your fabric too much. When finished, press the seams

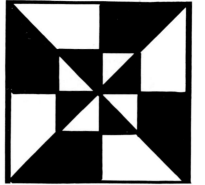

Illus. 8–3.

toward the darker color. Now form the Double Windmill pattern (Illus. 8–3) according to the photograph on p. 63 and the drawing on p. 61. For the next step, take a 4-inch strip of Color A, place it faceup on your machine and lay a completed block facedown on the strip. Sew the length of the strip and butt in all but five of the blocks, adding new strips as necessary. Then cut the blocks apart (Illus. 8–4).

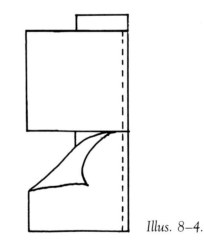

Illus. 8–4.

Sew four blocks together so that they look like Illus. 8–5. The five set aside blocks will go on the end of each row. Each row should consist of four blocks and three spacers, one between each block. Next, add joiner strips between each block using the same method as that used for the spacers.

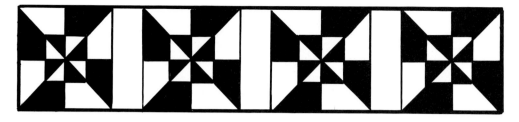

Illus. 8–5.

Finally, make your borders by first adding the five 3 × 45-inch strips of Color A and then those of Color B. Then add the other borders and finish using whichever method you prefer.

9
Trip Around the World

You will need eight colors for Trip Around the World but you don't need very much fabric for each. The pattern looks complex, but all it entails is sewing several groups of strips together.

YARDAGE

Colors A–H	¾ yard from each color
First border	⅞ yard
Second border	1½ yards
Third border	2 yards
Backing	5½ yards

CUTTING

Colors A–H	cut nine strips at $3\frac{1}{2} \times 16$ inches each
First border	cut eight strips at $3\frac{1}{2} \times 45$ inches
Second border	cut eight strips at $4\frac{1}{2} \times 45$ inches
Third border	cut nine strips at $5\frac{1}{2} \times 45$ inches

SEWING INSTRUCTIONS

Arrange your fabrics from light to dark and pin a small swatch of each next to the appropriate letter on the worksheet. This will give you a handy reference guide while you are sewing.

A	B	C	D	E	F	G	H
B	C	D	E	F	G	H	A
C	D	E	F	G	H	A	B
D	E	F	G	H	A	B	C
E	F	G	H	A	B	C	D
F	G	H	A	B	C	D	E
G	H	A	B	C	D	E	F
H	A	B	C	D	E	F	G
A	B	C	D	E	F	G	H

Now you can sew your strips into sheets. Referring to both your worksheet and to Illus. 9–1, sew your strips together along their lengths in the following order: A B C D E F G H A. Then press the seams toward the darkest colors. Pin a small sheet of paper to this sheet and label it Sheet 1. Set aside.

Next, sew seven more sheets in the same manner as described above.

Sheet 2: B C D E F G H A B
Sheet 3: C D E F G H A B C
Sheet 4: D E F G H A B C D
Sheet 5: E F G H A B C D E
Sheet 6: F G H A B C D E F
Sheet 7: G H A B C D E F G
Sheet 8: H A B C D E F G H

Press each sheet so that the seams are toward the darker colors.

For the next step, you should first look at Illus. 9–2. Then measure down 3½ inches from the top of your sewn sheet one. Make sure that the line you just marked is 3½ inches all the way across the sheet. Now cut across that line. You should now have a strip of squares. Continue to measure and cut strips until you have four strips of squares from sheet one. Stack these in a pile and mark them with the Sheet 1 label. Now cut Sheet 2 in the same manner. Cut the rest of the sheets and stack them, making sure to label each stack for easy identification.

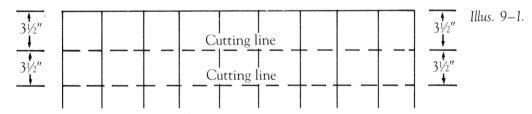

Illus. 9–1.

Your sheets were cut horizontally and now you will sew them together vertically. Use your worksheet and Illus. 9–3 as a guide. The letters indicated in Illus. 9–3 are the last three blocks in each strip. They are there to give you a visual aid in piecing the quilt. That is why the rest of the blocks were not drawn in. Sew together all of the strips that are shown in the illustration and then do the same with a second set of strips. These blocks will form the upper and lower halves of your quilt.

A	H	G	F	E	D	C	B	C	D	E	F	G	H	A
H	G	F	E	D	C	B	A	B	C	D	E	F	G	H
G	F	E	D	C	B	A	H	A	B	C	D	E	F	G
Strip from Sheet 1	Strip from Sheet 8	Strip from Sheet 7	Strip from Sheet 6	Strip from Sheet 5	Strip from Sheet 4	Strip from Sheet 3	Strip from Sheet 2	Strip from Sheet 3	Strip from Sheet 4	Strip from Sheet 5	Strip from Sheet 6	Strip from Sheet 7	Strip from Sheet 8	Strip from Sheet 1

Illus. 9–2.

You should have left over 2 strips from Sheet 1. You will use these to make your center block. First, remove a square A from its place next to square H, as shown in Illus. 9–4. Then remove both of the A squares from the second strip, as shown in Illus. 9–5.

Now sew the strips together so that the squares are in the following order:

H G F E D C B A B C D E F G H

See Illus. 9–6 for a visual guide.

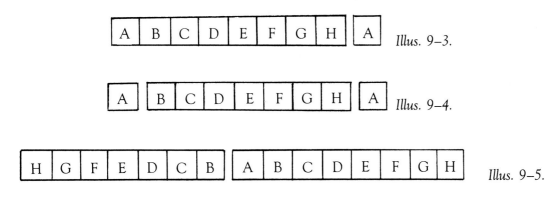

A	B	C	D	E	F	G	H		A

Illus. 9–3.

A		B	C	D	E	F	G	H		A

Illus. 9–4.

H	G	F	E	D	C	B		A	B	C	D	E	F	G	H

Illus. 9–5.

Next, sew the center row to the upper half, making sure to match up the seams on the squares. Then join the center row to the lower half. Attach the borders and finish the quilt according to whichever method you prefer.

10
Lover's Knot

Lover's Knot uses the double-nine-patch pattern as the basis of its block arrangements. Fabric choices are easy—you need only find suitable colors in light and dark contrasting shades.

YARDAGE

White fabric	3½ yards
Dark fabric	3½ yards
Backing	5½ yards

CUTTING

Please read "Speed Techniques" and "Rotary Cutter" in the front of this book before you start.

White fabric	cut thirty-three strips at 1½ × 45 inches
	cut ten strips at 4½ × 45 inches
	cut eight strips at 3 × 45 inches
Dark fabric	cut sixteen squares at 6 × 6 inches
	cut twenty-six strips at 1½ × 45 inches
	cut eight strips at 2 × 45 inches

SEWING INSTRUCTIONS

Lay a 1½-inch white strip faceup on the machine and a 6-inch square facedown on the strip. Sew down the length of the square

The type of borders pictured here, known as Amish Brothers, are built onto the quilt. They are first added to the sides of the quilt and then to the top and bottom. They are never mitered.

and butt in the next square. Continue this process until you have attached all of the white squares. Next, without doing any cutting, sew a 1½-inch dark strip to the white strip.

Finally, sew another 1½-inch white strip to the dark strip, press all of the seams, and cut the ends of the strips so that they are even with the block, as shown in Illus. 10–1. Then sew and cut the opposite side of the square in the same way and press the seams.

Next, sew a 1½-inch white strip to a 1½-inch dark strip along their entire lengths. Repeat this five times. Then add another white strip to the other side of a dark strip. Even off the ends of the strips, measure down 6 inches and cut a rectangle. Continue to measure and cut rectangles until you have thirty-two of them. Do not throw away the excess fabric because you'll need it for the next section.

For this part, see Illus. 10–2. Sew six sets of 1½-inch strips in a dark-white-dark combination (Set A). Then sew three sets of 1½-inch strips in a white-dark-white combination (Set B).

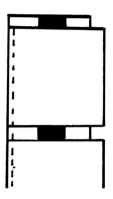

Illus. 10–1.

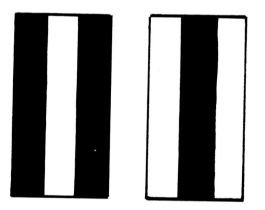

Illus. 10–2.

From Set A, cut one hundred and twenty-eight 1½-inch-long sections. From Set B, cut sixty-four 1½-inch-long sections. Sew the blocks to form a nine-block square, as shown in Illus. 10–3. Sew one of these blocks to each end of all of your 6-inch

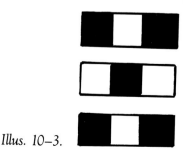

Illus. 10–3.

rectangles and sew each of these sections to the top and bottom of your squares as shown in Illus. 10-4.

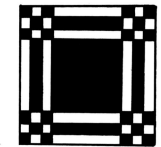

Illus. 10-4.

Illus. 10-5.

Next, take a 4½-inch white strip, place it faceup on your machine, and lay a completed block facedown on top of the strip. Sew the length of the block and butt in the subsequent blocks (Illus. 10-5) until the strip is full. Do the same to a second strip. When you are finished, cut the blocks and strips free.

Sew your blocks together according to Illus. 10-6. This will form the rows of your quilt. There should be four blocks in each row. Sew the remaining white strips to the blocks so that they form strips between each of the rows. Sew the 3-inch border strips together in pairs at their ends. Do the same with the 2-inch border strips. Sew the white border to the top and bottom and then to the sides. Do the same with the colored border.

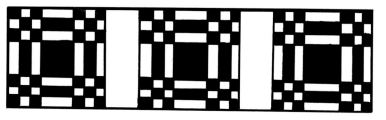

Illus. 10-6.

11
French Braid

The French Braid requires fabric in five different colors. Although it may look difficult to sew, it is actually quite easy, because you don't create the chevron pattern until the end.

YARDAGE

Colors A–E	1¼ yards (various colors)
First border	¾ yard (light color)
Second border	1 yard (medium color)
Third border	1½ yards (dark color)

CUTTING

Please read "Speed Techniques" and "Rotary Cutter" in the front of this book before you start.

Colors A–E	cut into as many 2½×45-inch strips as you can and then cut strips into 5-inch-long and 7-inch-long rectangles, alternating each measure along the length of the strip
First border	cut eight strips at 3×45 inches
Second border	cut eight strips at 4×45 inches
Third border	cut eight strips at 5×45 inches

SEWING INSTRUCTIONS

Lay a 7-inch rectangle right side up on your sewing machine. Take a 5-inch rectangle of the same color and lay it right side

down on the 7-inch rectangle so that the 2½-inch side of the 5-inch rectangle butts against the long side of the 7-inch rectangle (see Illus. 11–1). Sew together.

Take a 5-inch rectangle of the next darkest color and butt it against the side of the sewn set, as shown in Illus. 11–2. Sew the pieces together. Add a 7-inch rectangle of the same color to the 7-inch side of the first sewn set, as shown in Illus. 11–3. Continue adding rectangles in the appropriate colors until you have completed 25 sets. This is called a braid. Sew all of your rectangles together in the same manner until you have completed 10 braids. Press the seams well.

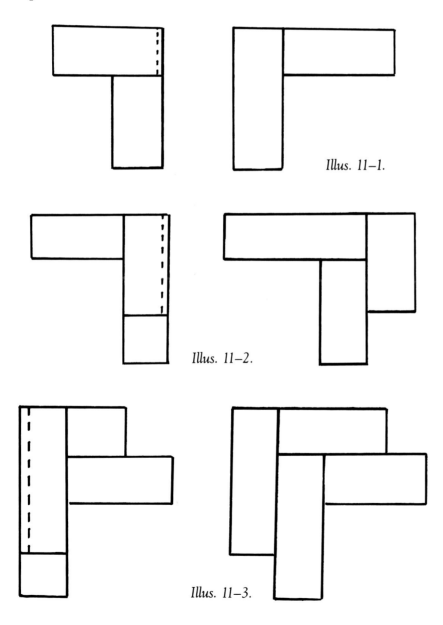

Illus. 11–1.

Illus. 11–2.

Illus. 11–3.

Now you will even up your braids. First, measure down ¼ inch from the point on the second set in your braid. Cut straight across, removing most of the first set. Then lay your ruler across the last set, lining it up with the end points on the second to last set and the bottom center point (see Illus. 11–4). Cut here as well.

To sew your braids together, measure ¼ inch in from the zig-zag sides on each braid and sew them together along this line, as indicated in Illus. 11–5. It is very important to stitch these sections accurately.

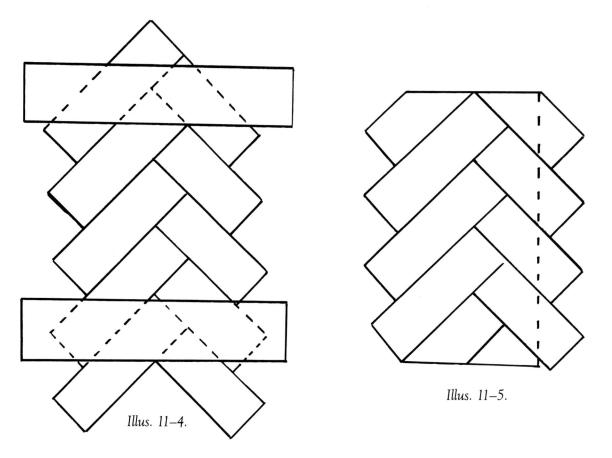

Illus. 11–4.

Illus. 11–5.

Next, sew the short ends of the borders together so that your eight 45-inch strips become four 90-inch strips. When you have completed this step, then sew the borders to the sides of your block of braids. Sew entirely along each side and cut the ends of the border strips to match the length of the braids. Sew the next two borders onto the first border. After you have added all of your borders, you can finish your quilt using whichever method you prefer.

12
Double Wedding Ring

This quilt was traditionally made by a bride-to-be right before her wedding and was to be used on her marriage bed. You may choose color combinations to suit any occasion or decor.

YARDAGE

Color A	2¼ yards (should be white)
Colors B–F	½ yard

CUTTING

Please read "Speed Techniques" and "Rotary Cutter" in the front of this book before you start.

Color A	cut twelve center pieces (use pattern on p. 87; make sure to include markers) cut thirty-one ovals (use pattern on p. 86)
Colors B–F	cut five strips at 2½ × 45 inches cut sixty-two joining squares—12 each from three colors and 13 each from two colors (use pattern on p. 87).

SEWING INSTRUCTIONS

Sew together one strip each of colors B–F in any order that you like. You will end up with five sets of strips. Press the seams.

Then, use the pattern on p. 86 to cut out 62 arches from the sheets, making sure to cut out the center markers.

Next, match each marker on each center piece to each outside marker on each arch. Pin them together and sew according to Illus. 12–1. Then match the inside marker on each arch to the

Make one   Make five   Make six   *Illus. 12–1.*

corresponding marker on one side of each oval (Illus. 12–2). Pin them together and sew. Then match center markers on the other side of each oval to their corresponding markers on the remaining arches (Illus. 12–3) and sew them together. Keep in mind that the illustrations show whole circles but not all of your circles are whole ones. Finally, add a joiner square to each end of the paired arches according to Illus. 12–4.

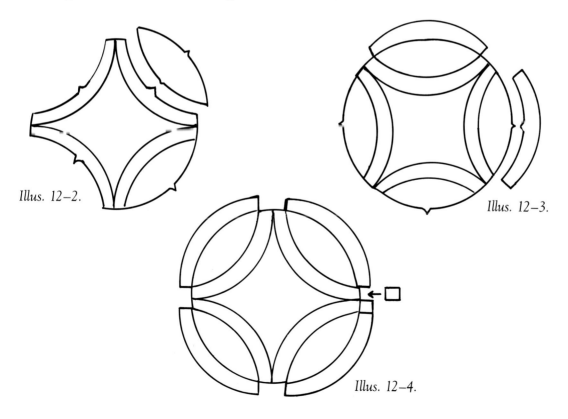

Illus. 12–2.

Illus. 12–3.

Illus. 12–4.

When you have completed that step, you will be ready to put your quilt together. Use the diagram in Illus. 12–5 to connect your sections to each other. Once your quilt has been pieced together, you can square off the corners and even off the sides by adding fabric to fill in around the rings. You may also choose to bind the edges as they are to produce a scalloped edge. Then finish the quilt by whichever method you prefer.

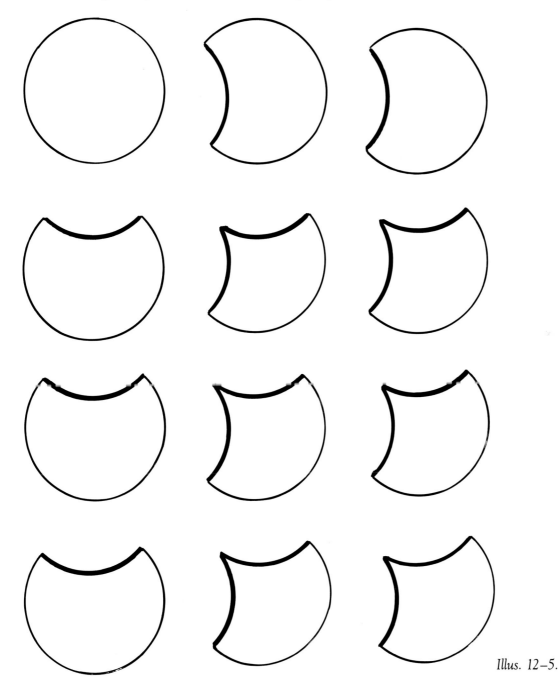

Illus. 12–5.

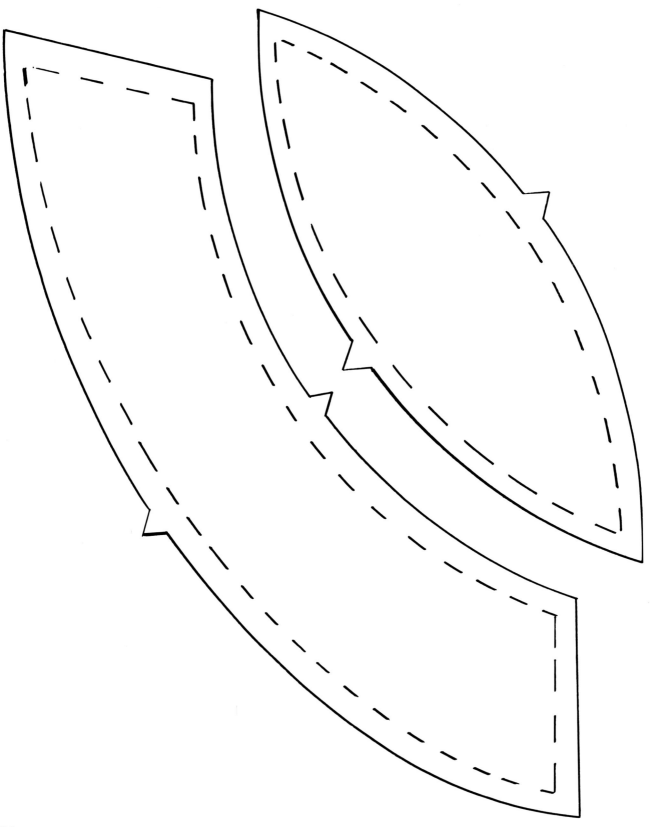

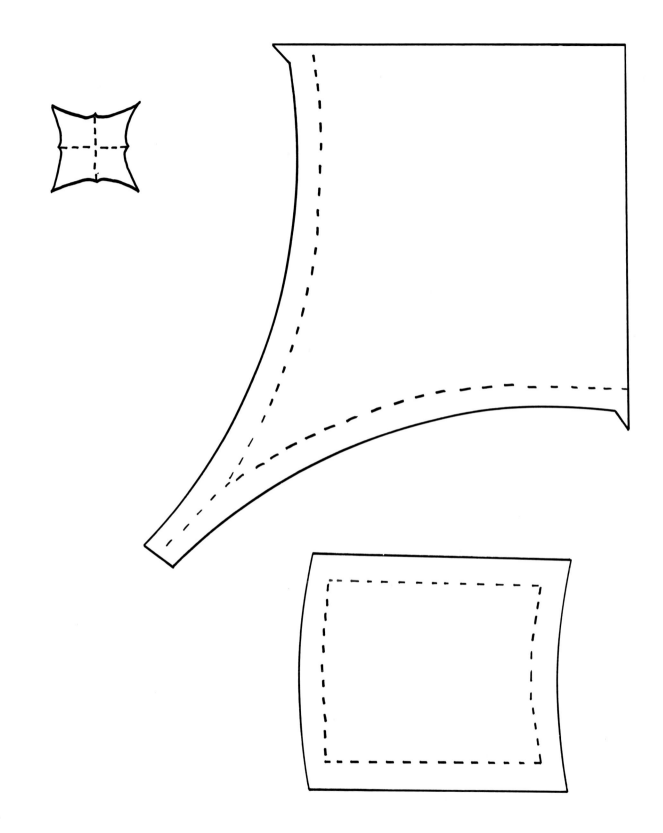

In colonial America, young girls were taught the art of quilting at a very young age. And by the time a girl reached marriageable age, she was expected to have finished at least twelve quilts. The last one had to be her wedding quilt, usually in this pattern. For this quilt, the bride-to-be would do the piecing and the friends and family would do the quilting.

13
Split Rail

The Split Rail requires eight different colors in varying degrees of light and dark for blocks of four strips each. However, if you use only five different colors, you can make strips of three colors each and form the Triple Rail pattern. I prefer the Split Rail because it is more colorful.

YARDAGE

Colors A–H	¾ yard
First border	1 yard
Second border	1 yard
Third border	2 yards

CUTTING

Please read "Speed Techniques" and "Rotary Cutter" in the front of this book before you start.

Colors A–H	cut eight strips at 2 × 45 inches
First border	cut eight strips at 4 × 45 inches
Second border	cut eight strips at 5 × 45 inches
Third border	cut eight strips at 6 × 45 inches

SEWING INSTRUCTIONS

Choose four colors that run from light to dark and sew them together in that order. Then sew the remaining four colors into blocks that also run from light to dark. Press them with their seams toward the darkest colors.

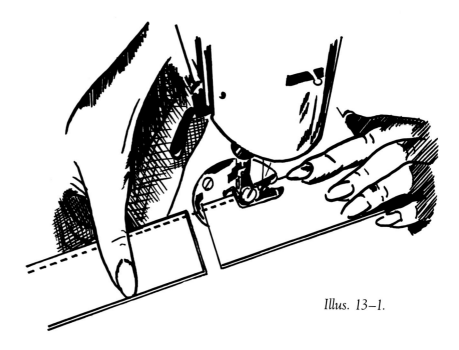

Illus. 13–1.

Measure one of your fabric combinations—it should be approximately an 8-inch square. If it is not, then cut it to that measure. Use this block as a template to cut the rest of your combinations. You should get thirty-two squares from each of your color combinations. Sew the blocks together as shown in Illus. 13–1 and finish the quilt using whatever method you prefer.

This is the traditional arrangement of blocks for the Split Rail quilt. You can change the arrangement to suit your own tastes, however.

Illus. 13–2.

14
Court House Steps

Court House Steps is a variation of the Log Cabin pattern (p. 31). However, it is constructed from pairs of strips of equal lengths rather than built up from strips of increasing lengths.

YARDAGE

Medium color	¼ yard (for center strip)
Light color A	½ yard
Light color B	⅝ yard
Light color C	⅞ yard
Dark color A	⅝ yard
Dark color B	⅞ yard
Dark color C	1¼ yards
Border	1¼ yards
Backing	5½ yards

CUTTING

Please read "Speed Techniques" and "Rotary Cutter" in the front of this book before you start.

Medium color	cut two strips at 2½ × 45 inches
Light color A	cut four strips at 2½ × 45 inches
Light color B	cut seven strips at 2½ × 45 inches
Light color C	cut ten strips at 2½ × 45 inches
Dark color A	cut seven strips at 2½ × 45 inches
Dark color B	cut ten strips at 2½ × 45 inches
Dark color C	cut fifteen strips at 2½ × 45 inches
Border	cut eight strips at 5 × 45 inches

SEWING INSTRUCTIONS

Lay one medium strip faceup on your machine. Lay one strip of light color A facedown on top of it and sew together. Do this with the second medium strip. Then, without doing any cutting, add a second strip of light color A to the other side of the medium strip. Press the seams away from the center strip.

Make sure that the three strips are even. Then measure down 2½ inches and cut as shown in Illus. 14–1. Continue to do this until you have twenty rectangles.

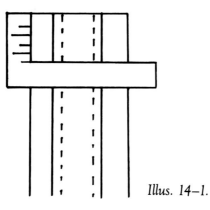

Illus. 14–1.

Take a strip of dark color A and lay it faceup on your machine. Lay a rectangle facedown on the strip, sew the length of the rectangle, and then butt in the next rectangle. Continue until all of your rectangles are finished. Cut the pieces so that the strips are even with the rectangle edges (Illus. 14–2).

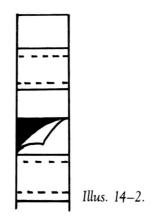

Illus. 14–2.

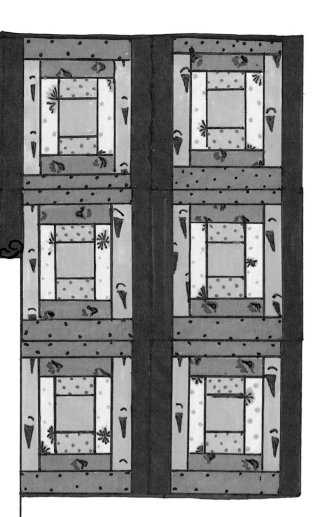

The block quilt has its origins in the United States. It was first used by quilters as they traveled across country in covered wagons. Because there was no room to set up a quilting loom, women would complete a quilt one block at a time and then piece the blocks together.

97

Take another dark color A strip and lay it faceup on your machine. Then lay one of the blocks you just completed facedown on the strip so that the other dark strip is on the opposite side of the block (see Illus. 14–3). Sew the pieces together and butt in new blocks until you have finished them all. Cut the blocks apart the same way as before.

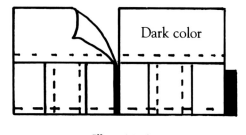

Illus. 14–3.

Lay a light color B strip faceup on your machine. Then lay one of the blocks facedown on the strip so that the dark strips are on the top and bottom of the block, as in Illus. 14–4. Sew the length of the block and butt in new blocks until they are all finished. Then cut your blocks free as before.

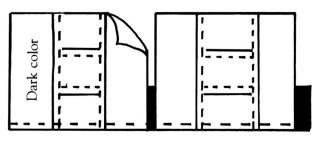

Illus. 14–4.

Lay a second light color B strip faceup on your machine and lay your block facedown on the strip so that the light strip you just added is opposite the new one. Sew the block to the strip and butt in the rest of the blocks.

Sew the remaining strips in the same manner, but attach the last light strips first and then the dark strips. Then sew the blocks together so that the last dark strips are at the sides. The quilt should be four blocks across and five blocks down.

Sew pairs of the border pieces together at their short ends; attach the pairs first to the top and bottom and then to the sides. Finish the quilt using whichever method you prefer.

15
Kaleidoscope

Kaleidoscope requires fabric in six colors, divided into contrasting pairs of light and dark shades. This quilt is very colorful and eye-catching—suitable for a child's room.

YARDAGE

Light color A	1½ yards
Light color B	1 yard (for corners, can be the same as light color A)
Medium light color	1½ yards
Medium dark color	1½ yards
Dark color A	1½ yards
Dark color B	1 yard (for corners, can be the same as dark color A)
Backing	6 yards

CUTTING

Please read "Speed Techniques" and "Rotary Cutter" in the front of this book before you start.

Light color A	cut fifteen strips at 2½ × 45 inches
Medium light color	cut fifteen strips at 2½ × 45 inches
Medium dark color	cut fifteen strips at 2½ × 45 inches
Dark color A	cut fifteen strips at 2½ × 45 inches
Light color B	cut thirty-two corners using pattern on p. 103
Dark color B	cut thirty-two corners using pattern on p. 103

SEWING INSTRUCTIONS

Sew fifteen sets of four strips each arranged from light to dark (Illus. 15–1). Press the sets with all the seams towards the darkest colors. Then lay the sets faceup on a flat surface and, using the triangle pattern on p. 103, draw as many triangles as you can (Illus. 15–2). You should get enough for one kaleidoscope with one triangle left over.

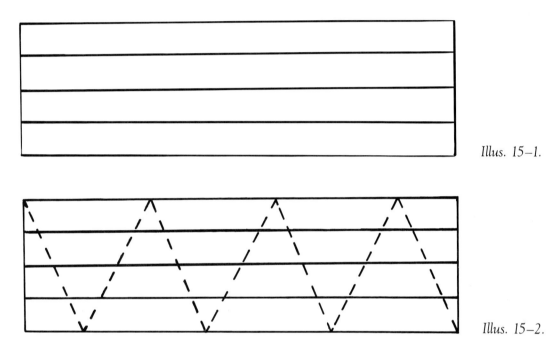

Illus. 15–1.

Illus. 15–2.

To begin your first kaleidoscope, sew together a triangle with a light point and a triangle with a dark point and repeat the step (Illus. 15–3). Now sew these two triangle sets together to form half of a kaleidoscope (Illus. 15–4). Repeat the process to form the other half of your kaleidoscope and sew the two halves together, making sure that the points line up nicely. Repeat these steps until you have 16 kaleidoscopes.

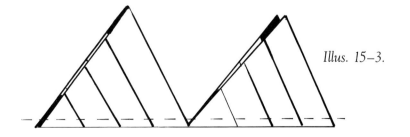

Illus. 15–3.

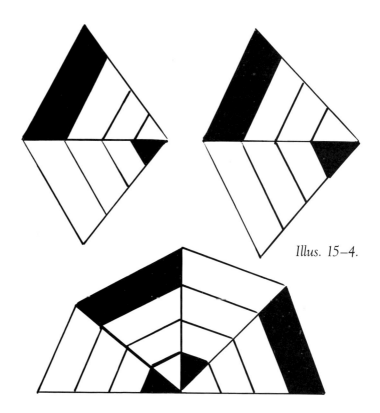

Illus. 15–4.

Next, you will attach the corners. On eight of the kaleidoscopes, attach dark corners to triangles with light bases. Then add light corners to dark bases on the other eight kaleidoscopes. Use Illus. 15–5 as a guide.

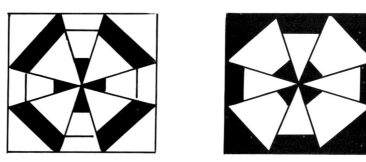

Illus. 15–5.

Finally, sew your squares together by alternating a square with light corners with a square with dark corners. You should arrange them in four rows of four squares each. By itself, this pattern makes a nice crib or lap quilt, but you can enlarge it by adding a suitable number of borders in appropriate colors.

Finish your quilt using whichever method you prefer.

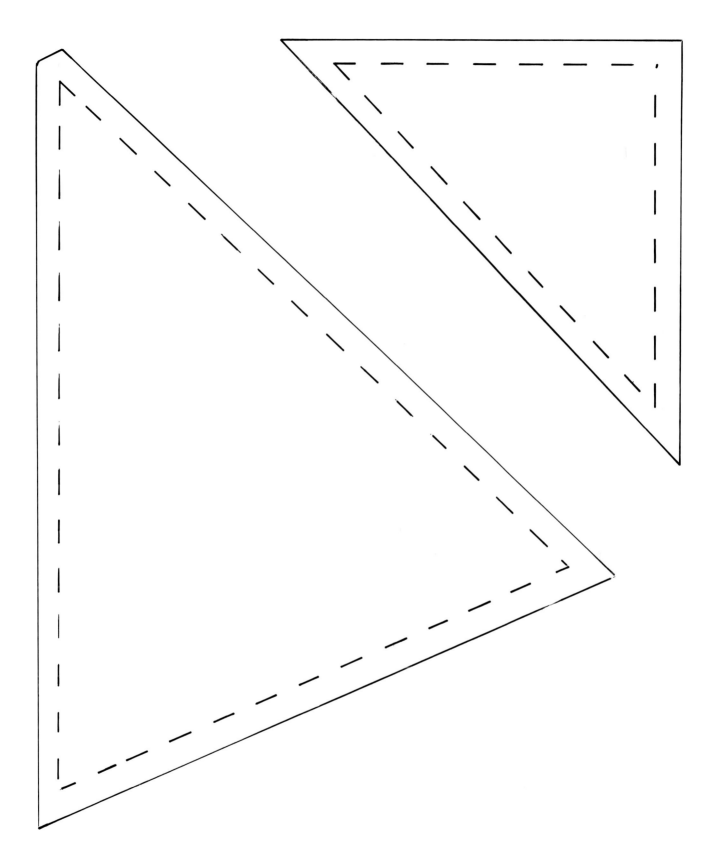

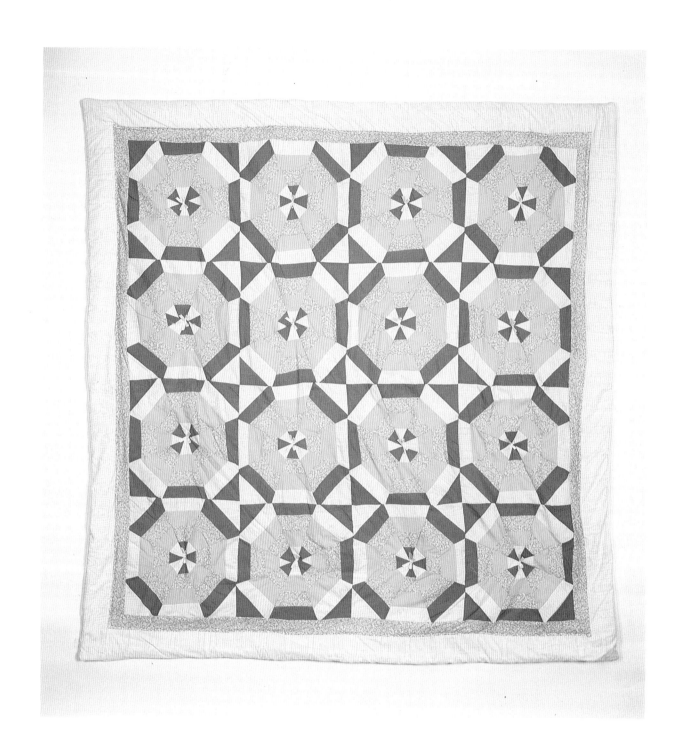

16
Hole in the Barn Door

Hole in the Barn Door is also commonly called Monkey Wrench or just Wrench. It is most usually associated with Amish and Mennonite quilters.

YARDAGE

Medium color	⅞ yard
White	1¾ yard (with or without print)
Light color	½ yard (center strip)
Medium dark color	1¾ yard (corner triangles)
Dark color	2 yards (solid squares)

CUTTING

Medium color	cut nine strips at $2\frac{1}{2} \times 45$ inches
White	cut nine strips at $2\frac{1}{2} \times 45$ inches (save remainder for triangles)
Light color	cut three strips at 4×45 inches
Dark color	cut fifteen squares at 12×12 inches
Medium dark color	save for triangles

SEWING INSTRUCTIONS

Sew your white and medium 2½-inch strips together in pairs lengthwise. It's easiest to butt each pair in rather than cut them apart as you sew. When done, press the seams toward the dark color.

Next, lay a sewn strip faceup on the machine with the dark color to the right. Then lay a 4-inch strip face down on top of it. Sew the length of the strips. Continue sewing until all the

4-inch strips are sewn to the paired strips. Press with seams toward the 4-inch strips.

Place a set of strips faceup on your machine with the 4-inch strip to the right. Place a sewn 2½-inch set facedown on top of the 4-inch strip with the darkest color to the right. Sew the length of the strips and press with the seams toward the darkest color.

When you have finished sewing, even off the top, measure down 4 inches and cut across (Illus. 16–1), making sure that the cut is even. Continue cutting until you have fifteen center strips. Do the same with the remaining sets of 2½-inch strips. Press the cut pieces and set them aside.

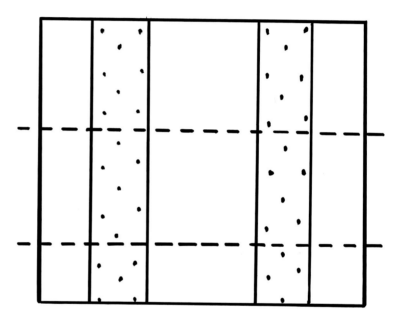

Illus. 16–1.

Place the remaining white and medium dark fabric together with right sides facing. Then mark a grid of 5×5-inch squares on the back of the dark fabric. Pin the two fabrics together and draw diagonal lines through the centers of the squares. Then follow the directions for sewing triangles on page 15. When done sewing, cut according to the same directions and press the seams toward the dark fabric.

Sew together a striped block and a triangle set (two half-square triangles) so that the dark triangle is on the inside (Illus. 16–2). Repeat until you have thirty combinations. Press all the seams toward the dark color. Then take a second triangle set and sew it to the other side of the striped block, again making

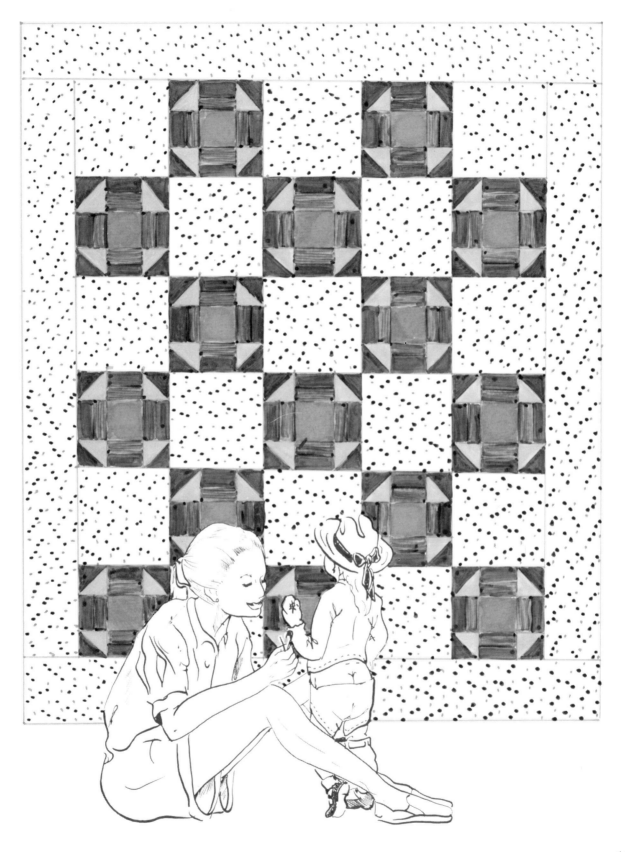

sure that the dark triangle is toward the striped block. Repeat this step twenty-nine more times and press the seams toward the dark color.

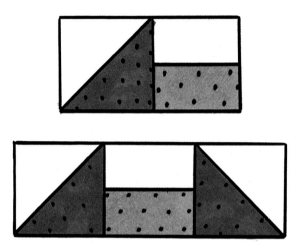

Illus. 16–2.

Next, sew two of the blocks that you just made to either side of a center strip so that your finished block looks like Illus. 16–3. This is one block in your quilt. Now complete fourteen more blocks.

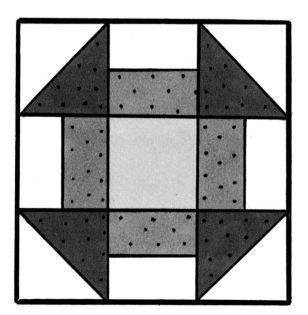

Illus. 16–3.

You can now put your quilt blocks together to form your quilt top. In all, your top will consist of six rows of five blocks each. Your first row should start with a "Barn Door" block, then a solid block, then another "Barn Door" block, then a solid block,

and end with a "Barn Door" block. The second row should be the reverse of that, and so on for six rows.

If you want to add borders, I have provided yardage for them below, but you may leave your quilt as it is if you like.

YARDAGE

First border	1¾ yards
Second border	1½ yards
Third border	2 yards

CUTTING

First border	cut eight strips at 3×45 inches
Second border	cut eight strips at 4×45 inches
Third border	cut eight strips at 5×45 inches

Sew the first border strips together at their short ends and apply the pieces first to the sides and then to the top and bottom of the quilt. Do the same with the second and third borders. Finish your quilt according to the method you like best.

17
Flowering Tulip

This quilt requires fabric in six colors. Flowering Tulip can be a very colorful quilt, adding a spring feeling to a room, no matter what the season.

YARDAGE

Light color	⅞ yard (for tulip)
Medium color	⅞ yard (for tulip)
White	1½ yards
Dark color	⅝ yard (base of tulips)
Medium light color	2¼ yards (for joiner strips and border)
Medium dark color	⅜ yard (for random squares)

CUTTING

Light color	cut ten strips at 2½ × 45 inches
Medium color	cut ten strips at 2½ × 45 inches
White	cut five strips at 3½ × 45 inches
	cut five strips at 4 × 45 inches
Dark color	cut three strips at 5 × 45 inches
Medium light color	cut five strips at 2½ × 45 inches
	cut three strips at 7 × 45 inches
	cut eight strips at 3 × 45 inches
Medium dark color	cut three strips at 2½ × 45 inches

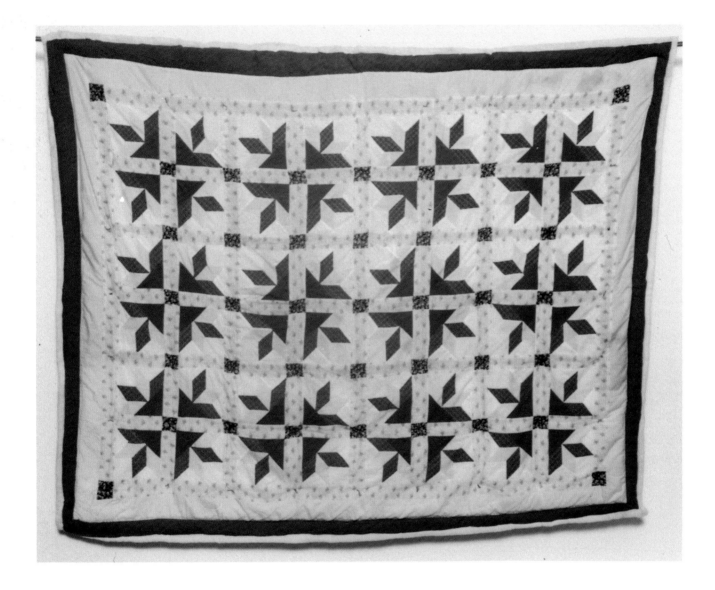

SEWING INSTRUCTIONS

The first step in this project will be making the tulips. First sew together in pairs the light and medium 2½-inch strips. Make sure that the darker color is on the bottom. It's best to chain-sew the strips by butting in a new one each time you finish one. **Do not** press them when you are done. They need to be cut first. Lay your strips down on a cutting mat, preferably one with a grid on it. If you are left-handed, then line the fabric up with one of the lines on the right side of the mat. If you are right-handed, then do the opposite. Then cut off the top of the strip at a 45° angle (Illus. 17–1). Then measure down 2½ inches and cut again. Repeat this until you have finished cutting all ten strips. Remember to continually check to see that your angle stays correct. You should have ninety-six single tulips when you finish cutting. Then you can press the seams toward the darker color and divide your tulips into two equal piles.

Next, you are going to work with your 3½-inch white strips and one pile of your tulips. First, place a 3½-inch strip faceup

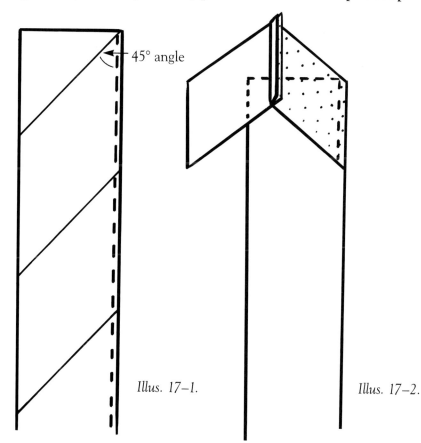

45° angle

Illus. 17–1.   *Illus. 17–2.*

on your machine and place a single tulip facedown on your white strip with the darkest fabric to the right (Illus. 17–2). Sew down the side until you come to the end of the tulip and then butt in another tulip. Continue this process until all of the tulips from your first pile are finished (Illus. 17–3).

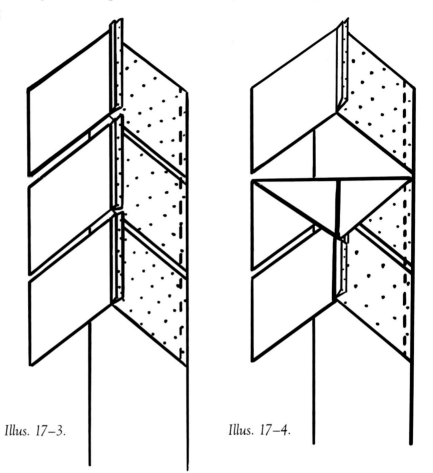

Illus. 17–3.

Illus. 17–4.

Even off the bottom of your 3½-inch strips and, starting from the top, fold down the point of the second tulip, as shown in Illus. 17–4. Then cut the white strip straight across on that line. Do this until all of your tulips are cut free. Press the seams toward the darkest color.

Now take one of the pieces that you have just sewn and place it faceup on your machine with the bottom righthand corner under the needle (Illus. 17–5). Place a tulip from the second pile facedown on top of the white square, as shown in Illus. 17–6. Make sure to leave ¼ inch of the tulip below the edge of the white square. Sew down the length of the tulip until you reach the point where the tulip and white square edges meet. With

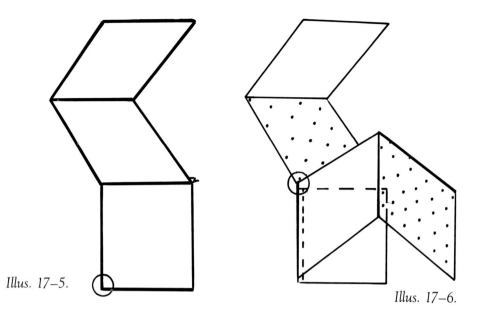

the needle still in the fabric, pivot the block so that you can sew the two connecting edges of the tulip together (Illus. 17–7). Press the seams flat. This is called a double tulip.

For the next step, take your 4-inch white strips and cut them into 4-inch white squares. Then cut the squares diagonally to form triangles. You'll need ninety-six triangles in all.

Lay a double tulip faceup on your machine with the far left point of your tulip under the needle. Place a triangle facedown on the tulip, leaving about ¼ inch over the edge of the seam of your tulip. Sew the length of your triangle and then, with the needle still in the fabric, pivot the block so that you can sew the other side of the triangle. Then sew a triangle in the same manner to the other side of the tulip. Continue the process until all of the tulips have triangles on either side of them (Illus. 17–8). Then press all the seams flat.

Next, you are going to work with your 5-inch medium dark strips. First cut them into 5-inch squares and then cut them on their diagonals to form forty-eight triangles. Sew a triangle to the base of a tulip block, as shown in Illus. 17–9. Then repeat the process with the rest of your tulip blocks. You should now set aside six squares until later.

Now you are going to join your blocks together. First take one of your 2½-inch joiner strips and lay it faceup on your machine. Then take one of the squares and lay it facedown on the joiner strip so that the base triangle is in the lower righthand corner. Sew the length of the square. Then butt in another square face-

Quilting has a long and illustrious history. In fact, the Cairo Museum in Egypt has in its collections a beautifully colored quilted canopy that dates from 960 B.C.

116

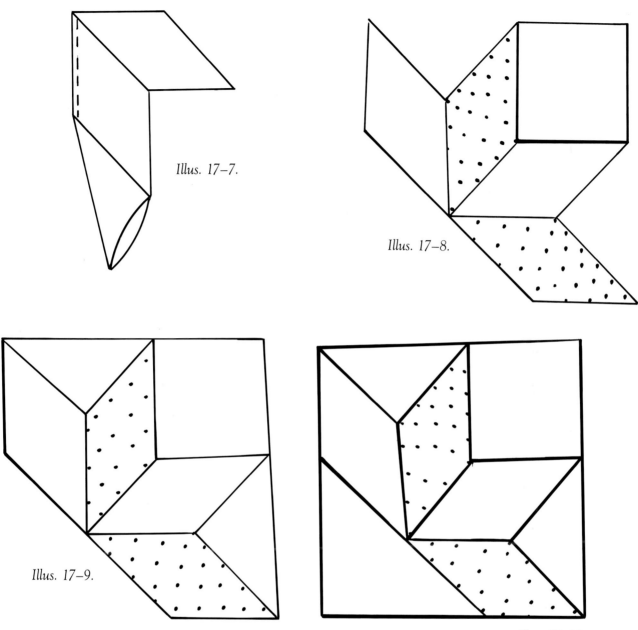

Illus. 17–7.

Illus. 17–8.

Illus. 17–9.

Illus. 17–10.

down, but this time arrange it so that the base triangle is in the lower lefthand corner. Sew the length of the square and butt in the rest of the triangles, remembering to alter the direction of the triangle each time (Illus 17–10). Then repeat the steps with the rest of the joiner strips and blocks. Then press down all the seams toward the squares. Now you can cut apart your blocks so that the joiner strips are even with the square edges.

Sew your rows, starting out with one of the set aside squares. You should make eight rows all together. Set them aside.

Now sew a joiner strip to a 2½-inch random square strip. Sew down the length and repeat the process with the remaining 7-inch joiner strips and the 2½-inch random square strips. Then cut them apart and sew them to look like Illus. 17–11. When finished, you should have a large sheet. Press with seams toward the darker color.

Illus. 17–11.

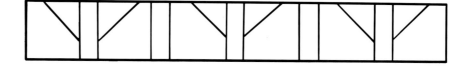

Now measure down 3 inches and cut all the way across the sheet. Repeat the measuring and cutting down the entire length of the sheet. You will need fourteen strips in all.

Sew two of your strips together along their 3-inch ends. Then attach another strip to one end of the sewn strips. Continue to sew pairs of strips until you have seven very long strips. Remove the last square so that your ends are two 7-inch blocks. Now use the strips to form dividers between your tulip-block rows.

Last, you'll make the borders. Take two 3 × 45-inch strips of medium light color and sew the short ends together to form long strips. Do the same with the rest of the first border strips. Then join the strips to the sides and then the top and bottom of your quilt. Do the same with the second and third borders. I love the look of three borders on this quilt because of the wonderful framing effect.

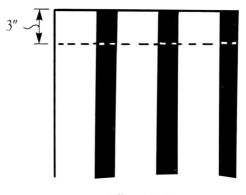

3″

Illus. 17–12.

18
Hundreds of Triangles

By using strip-quilting techniques, this quilt, which would take months to piece by hand, can be made in only a few hours.

YARDAGE

Colors A–G	1 yard each
Color H	¾ yard (for top, bottom, and sides only)
Backing	6 yards

CUTTING

Please read "Speed Techniques" and "Rotary Cutter" in the front of this book before you start.

Colors A–G	cut six strips from each of the fabrics at 5 × 45 inches
Color H	cut two strips at 5 × 45 inches cut eighteen long triangles (use pattern on p. 125, set aside rest of Color H until later in the project)

SEWING INSTRUCTIONS

To begin, take any one of the 5 × 45-inch strips and sew it lengthwise to a strip in another color. It does not matter which color combination you choose. Use twelve to fourteen stitches

per inch for this project. Then butt in a new set of strips and sew that together. Continue to do this until all of your strips are paired. Then cut the sets apart, as shown in Illus. 18–1.

Next, sew the other side of each set of strips, butting in a new set each time you finish one (Illus. 18–2). When finished, cut the sets apart. You should have twenty-one sets in all.

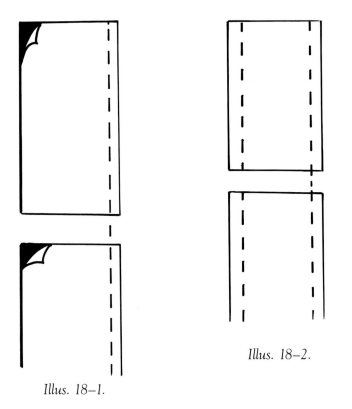

Illus. 18–1.

Illus. 18–2.

Now lay three of the sets one on top of the other and make sure that the edges line up and that the fabric is smooth. Then, using the triangle pattern on p. 125, mark the fabric as indicated in Illus. 18–3 and use your rotary cutter to cut out the required number of triangles. You should get thirteen triangles from each sewn strip. Repeat the above steps to cut the rest of your sewn strips.

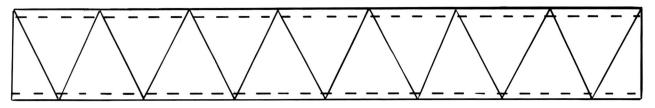

Illus. 18–3.

When you have completed your cutting, you should have sets of triangles that are attached at their bases. The sewing at their tops will come out easily, so open them up and press them with the seams toward the darker fabric. From here on, each pair of triangles will be referred to as a set.

For this step, take the two 5×45-inch strips of Color H and lay one on top of the other with their right sides together. Then cut them into triangles according to the instructions above without sewing them together. With the rest of Color H, cut out six more triangles. You will end up with a total of 32 triangles.

With the leftover Fabric H, make 16 long triangles, using the pattern on p. 125 and your rotary cutter.

Now we can start the fun part—sewing the quilt. We will do this diagonally, not up and down or across. The instructions will be given one row at a time.

Row 1:   Take a single triangle and sew it to
                            a long triangle (both are cut from
                            Color H). Make sure that the base
                            of the single triangle is placed so
                            that it will be at the top after it is
                            sewn and opened up (Illus. 18-4).

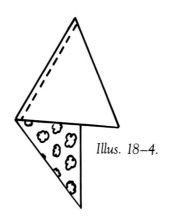

Illus. 18-4.

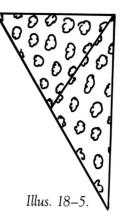

Illus. 18-5.

Row 2:   Sew together a single triangle, two
                            triangle sets, and a long triangle
                            (see Illus. 18-5).

Row 3:   Sew together a single triangle, four
                            triangle sets, and a long triangle.

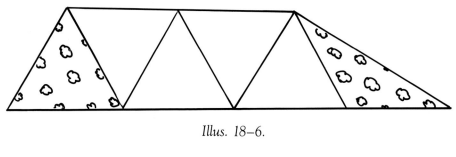

Illus. 18–6.

Row 4:	Sew together a single triangle, six triangle sets, and a long triangle.
Row 5:	Sew together a single triangle, eight triangle sets, and a long triangle.
Row 6:	Sew together a single triangle, ten triangle sets, and a long triangle.
Row 7:	Sew together a single triangle, twelve triangle sets, and a long triangle.
Row 8:	Sew together a single triangle, fourteen triangle sets, and a long triangle.
Row 9:	Sew together a single triangle, sixteen triangle sets, and a long triangle.
Rows 10–17:	For each row, sew together a single triangle, sixteen triangle sets, and another single triangle (see Illus. 18–6).

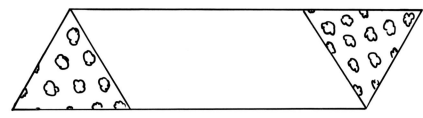

Illus. 18–7.

124

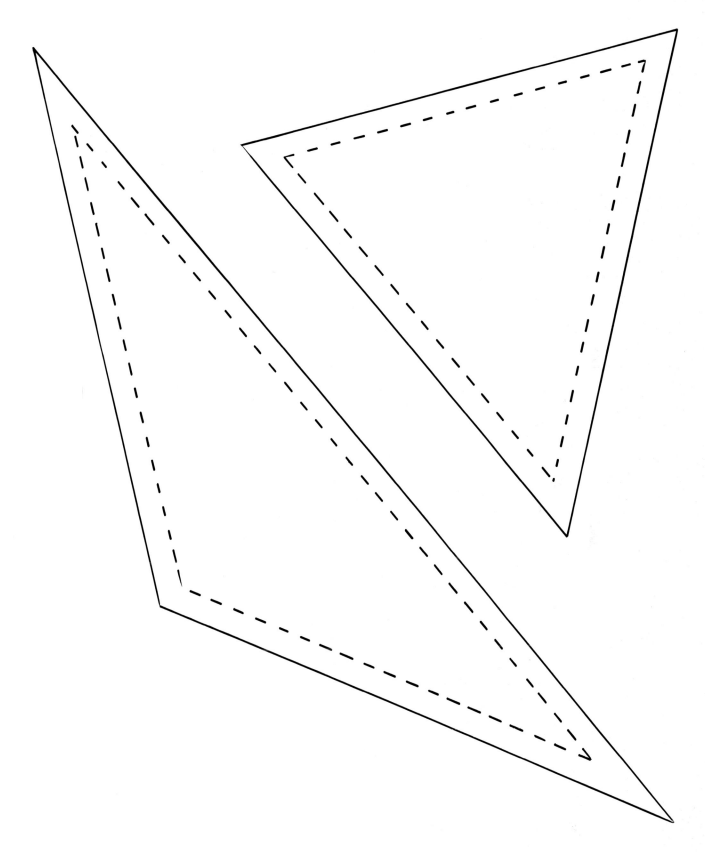

Row 18:	Sew together a long triangle, fourteen triangle sets, and a single triangle.
Row 19:	Sew together a long triangle, twelve triangle sets, and a single triangle.
Row 20:	Sew together a long triangle, ten triangle sets, and a single triangle.
Row 21:	Sew together a long triangle, eight triangle sets, and a single triangle.
Row 22:	Sew together a long triangle, six triangle sets, and a single triangle.

Illus. 18–8. Placement of long and single triangles.

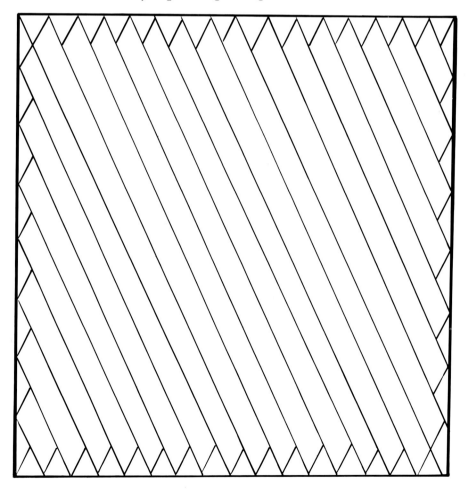

Row 23:	Sew together a long triangle, four triangle sets, and a single triangle.
Row 24:	Sew together a long triangle, two triangle sets, and a single triangle.
Row 25:	Sew together a long triangle and a single triangle.

At this point, you may choose to either leave your quilt as it is or add borders. If you choose to add borders, you should probably choose a fabric identical or similar to one used in the body of your quilt. Yardage amounts for borders are provided below.

First border	¾ yard cut into eight strips at 3 × 45 inches
Second border	1 yard cut into eight strips at 4 × 45 inches
Third border	1½ yards cut into eight strips at 5 × 45 inches

Pair off your strips and sew together on their short ends. Then sew the first border to the sides and then the top and bottom of your quilt. Do the same with the second and third borders. Finish by whatever method you prefer.

I hope you enjoy your quilting. Don't stop here—there are many other wonderful patterns out there to enjoy. Have fun!

INDEX